240
Mai

Reflections for busy people

....

John D. Jess
CHAPEL OF THE AIR

....

compiled by Faith Jess Mains

Tyndale House Publishers, Inc.   Wheaton, Illinois

First printing, December 1981

Library of Congress Catalog Card Number 81-84990
ISBN 0-8423-5399-2, paper

CONTENTS

PREFACE

Most books come into being through the diligent writing and rewriting of the author and the assistance of an editor or two. Such was not the case in the compiling of this material. These excerpts were painstakingly extracted from scores of my original radio manuscripts by my sister, Faith Mains, as a labor of love. To her belongs all the credit for their compilation and publication.

It is my sincere prayer that these gleanings will bring you the same inspiration and joy I received in their research and preparation some years ago. If that is the case, this recycling effort will have been well worthwhile.

John D. Jess

1 THE URGENCY OF THE PRESENT

Forgetting those things which are behind, and reaching forth unto those things which are before, I press toward the mark. . . .
Philippians 3: 13, 14

We are all acquainted with people who are always *going* to do something. It's not that they don't *intend* to accomplish it someday, but they just haven't found time to do it . . . yet.

"Now it is high time to awake out of sleep," Paul reminded the Christians in Rome, "for now is our salvation nearer than when we believed" Rom. 13:11.

Just where are you living, Christian friend? If you are all wrapped up in the past, isn't that foolish? Those "good old days" can never be recalled. You can't bring back yesterday's joys; neither can you rectify its mistakes. God tells His children to forget the past. Move on!

But perhaps your sights are fixed only on the future. If so, you are neglecting the importance of today. When Paul said he was "reaching unto those things which are before," he meant he was using *today's hours* in anticipation of the days to come. "*This* is the day which the Lord hath made; we will rejoice and be glad in *it!*"

John Haggai, in his book *How to Win Over Worry,* says:

Yesterday is a cashed check and cannot be negotiated. Tomorrow is a promissory note and cannot be utilized today. Today is cash in hand. Spend it wisely.

At the beginning of a brand New Year, I can think of no better reminder of the importance of the present.

For every one that asketh receiveth; and he that seeketh findeth; and to him that knocketh it shall be opened. Luke 11:10

I confess I don't understand exactly why God wants us to pray with stubborn persistence (importunity), but I know that certain things happen when we do — things that wouldn't have happened otherwise.

In Luke 11, Jesus related a parable that underscores the necessity of importunate prayer. A certain man knocked on his friend's door at midnight to ask for some bread to feed an unexpected guest. Although the sleepy neighbor told him to go away, the man continued to knock and ask, and his petition was eventually granted.

There is valuable spiritual therapy in asking God importunately for what we need. Of course He could provide the need before we ask, but that's not in our best interest. We need the communion that comes through prayer, the patience that comes with waiting for the answer, and the faith that is an integral part of continuing to ask.

And sometimes we need the discernment that comes with having to honestly separate our wants from our needs.

Here are three helpful prerequisites to importunate prayer.

1. The prayer must be a legitimate one. God doesn't answer frivolous petitions.
2. The prayer cannot be casual. It must be desperate.
3. Don't play games with God. If you are genuinely concerned for that loved one, don't pray just once for him or her. *Keep on knocking!*

Prayer is not just an easy way of getting what you want, but the only way of becoming what God wants us to be.

Godliness with contentment is great gain. 1 Timothy 6:6

Seneca, the Roman Stoic philosopher, once said: "If you would make a man happy, do not add to his possessions, but subtract from his desires."

I agree. One of the most frequently missing ingredients today, even among some Christians, is peace of mind. I'm referring to the kind of peace that stems from knowing *who* you are and *why* you are, and being satisfied in both categories.

Because *things* do not produce contentment on a permanent basis, this kind of peace is virtually extinct in today's society. Neither is it attained through forms of meditation or thought erasure. Why? Because contentment springs from the inward condition of the heart.

How then is contentment acquired?

First, you must desire it above all else. It will never be forced upon you, even by God.

Second, it must be received from our Savior, Jesus Christ, who said: "Peace I leave with you; my peace I give you. I do not give to you as the world gives. Do not let your hearts be troubled, and do not be afraid" John 14:27 NIV.

This peace is born and bred in the knowledge of sins forgiven, Fatherly watch-care throughout every step of life's journey, and the sure knowledge that when this life is finished, there remains an eternity of peace.

And be ye kind one to another, tenderhearted, forgiving one another, even as God for Christ's sake has forgiven you. Ephesians 4:32

Frederick William Faber, the 19th-century English Roman Catholic clergyman and hymn writer, penned these words:

Kind words are the music of the world. They have a power which seems to be beyond natural causes, as if they were some angel's song which had lost its way and come down to earth. It seems as if they could almost do what in reality God alone can do — soften the hard and angry hearts of men.

What would you like to be most remembered for after you are gone? Your philanthropies, your intellect, your inventiveness, your scientific or technological adroitness? Let me share my dearest wish, although it may be too late. I would like to be remembered most for my *kindness.*

It was said of Henry Ward Beecher that no one ever felt the full force of his kindness until he did Beecher an injury. What a coveted epitaph!

I gather, from the teaching of Scripture, that kindness is much more than a cultivated grace; instead, it is a byproduct of the love God implants in the hearts of His people for their fellow believers and the unconverted. "Be ye *kindly* affectioned one to another with brotherly love," we read in Romans 12:10.

A little girl who had just received a merciless tongue-lashing from her mother was heard to sob, "I wish mother loved me as much as she does God. She talks so kind to Him!"

For God sent not his Son into the world to condemn the world; but that the world through him might be saved. John 3:17

It is impossible to love people unless we first love Him who loved them and gave Himself for them.

I think of the missionaries who genuinely love people of other cultures, of other ethnic backgrounds; people with skin color differing from theirs. Thousands have buried their lives in steaming jungles to witness to these people, living among them, suffering with them, ministering to them.

How easy it is for us to withdraw from such people, to be repulsed by them, and to consider ourselves "in step" while they are "out of step." But when we love Christ with all our hearts, that attitude not only changes — it becomes impossible!

This does not mean we endorse everything such people do. Jesus loved the world, but He didn't endorse its sin. Where there was need, however, He was always there to help, to love, to bless, to heal, to save.

Many of us, I am sure, feel that we cannot — even should not — love those who are unlovable. But isn't that what the Christian life is all about? Anyone can love those who are lovable, but it takes a miracle to be able to love the unlovable.

An Ontario minister whose study had been burglarized several times tacked a sign on his door, which read:

Hi, Friend!
1. The money isn't here. Try the bank down the street.
2. Did you know that the Lord really loves you?
3. If I can help, please call me. My phone is _____

Apparently he knew quite a bit about loving the unlovable.

But whosoever will be great among you, shall be your minister.
Mark 10:43

Have you ever noticed how people exult when others recognize them
or call them by name? It's never a social blunder to make people feel
important.

But the passion to be noticed often gets out of hand. *Unsanctified
ego* pits man against man, group against group, nation against nation.
When a person begins to believe he or she is superior to others, a lot
of people are in for trouble because bigotry is a putrid by-product of an
inflated ego.

On the other hand, it isn't wrong to want to excel. The Christian's
greatest caution, however, must be in the area of *motives*. To feel
impelled to do good for a lot of people requires a certain amount of
ego (self-confidence), but God doesn't condemn that. Jesus gave
tremendous responsibility to His disciples, but He delineated the kind
of greatness He had in mind for them in Mark 10:43.

God made you and me to be greater than all the rest of His creation
combined, and the reason for this potential lies in the fact that human
beings alone have the ability to convey God's message of love to all
mankind.

Francis Bacon, Lord Chancellor of England in the early 17th century,
put it this way: "The desire of power caused the angels to fall; the
desire of knowledge in excess caused man to fall; but in love there is
no excess. Neither angel or man come in danger by it."

That, my friend, is the product of a God-directed, God-glorifying
ego, the loftiest ambition to which we can aspire.

7 PEACE

The fruit of the Spirit is . . . peace. Galatians 5:22

Those who seek a life wholly devoid of disturbing influences are grasping at smoke. But Jesus *did* promise peace to His followers — not as an end, but as a by-product.

The shallowness of our times is reflected in men's search for fruits without roots — the benefits of Christianity without having any part of Christianity. They want God's gifts without having to be bothered with Him!

But peace, my friend, is not a commodity you can purchase at the supermarket or variety store. It is the effect of *reconciliation* with God. Romans 5:1: "Therefore being justified by faith, we have *peace* with God through our Lord Jesus Christ." This is not the result of isolation from the world or of learning to put our minds in neutral or of living in perpetual positiveness. God, you see, doesn't bestow peace apart from His Son, who is Himself our peace (Ephesians 2:14).

Peace doesn't come from a full stomach or the accumulation of things, because human beings are a special, spiritual creation and their problems lie deeper than immediate physical needs. Mankind, alone out of all God's creation, has a heart need, and until that is satisfied, there can never be true and lasting peace.

I prayed for peace, and dreamed of restful ease,
  A slumber drugged from pain, a hushed repose;
Above my head the skies grew black with storm,
  And fiercer grew the onslaught of my foes;
But while the battle raged, and wild winds blew,
  I heard His voice, and perfect peace I knew.

Now is my soul troubled. And what shall I say? "Father, save me
from this hour"? No, for this purpose I have come to this hour.
John 12:27 RSV

Why me? The question surfaces most often when pain or tragedy
occurs in our lives. We can be very philosophical about the problem of
evil in the world but when it is *our* head that hurts, or when *our* heart
is breaking then comes the question, "Why must I be the one to suffer?
Why is this happening to *me?*"

Of course, the question is seldom asked on cloudless days. We
take most of life's good gifts for granted, assuming we deserve them.
But when the waters become troubled, when suffering and
disappointment mar the pastoral scene, we are ready to question the
Maker of it all, while moaning, "Why me?"

Perhaps you are asking that question today, and my answer is
simply, because you are a member of the human race, and you are
here. Many dedicated Christians are badly hurt, or obliged to go
through periods of prolonged suffering. Paul tells us in Romans 8 that
we wait for the redemption of our bodies, but until we experience that
bodily redemption, we will be subjected to the trials common to
mankind.

Moses asked the question, "Why me?" when God called him to
confront Pharaoh about those Israelite slaves. Have you reacted thus
to God's call? You know you should become involved in some of the
world's problems, but can't someone else do it — someone who
enjoys that sort of thing? Listen! There is in each of us a potential for
doing something beneficial. There are places where only *our* light
can shine — needs that only *our* hands can meet.

Why me? Because God has assigned a responsibility to you and
me that is ours alone. God has no duplications in His creation. There is
a darkness that only your light can dispel, a loneliness that only your
love can reach.

You have come to this hour for a purpose. That is the real answer
to the question, "Why me?"

9 HALF-HOURS THAT DETERMINE DESTINY

Are there not twelve hours in the day? If any man walk in the day, he stumbleth not, because he seeth the light of this world.
John 11:9

Have you ever considered how half-hours decide just about everything we do in life? Our biographies are made up of very short segments of time—the things we do and say in thirty-minute segments.

That half-hour we spend reading good or bad books, watching good or bad television programs, meditating on the things of God or seeking self-aggrandizement—these are the periods of our lives that determine whether we are good or bad: whether we are saved or lost!

How well I remember, so many years ago, the half-hour I tossed on my bed in the wee small hours of the morning, wrestling with my conscience. My decision for Christ took place within the space of half an hour, but it changed the course of my life.

There was the half-hour in which I decided, at the Holy Spirit's urging, to dedicate my life to the gospel ministry. Later there was another half-hour in which I said, "Yes," to God's prodding (against the advice of friends) to launch *The Chapel of the Air* radio broadcast.

Maybe you've been postponing your decision to receive Christ as your personal Savior. Right now God has given you another half-hour and it could be the most meaningful thirty minutes of your entire life!

Or do you need to use this half-hour to quietly submit to His leading? If so, wouldn't this be the ideal time to listen and respond to His voice and experience the spiritual therapy of obedience to His will?

The tongue is a fire, a world of iniquity . . . (it) setteth on fire the course of nature; and it is set on fire of hell. James 3:6

Child abuse has undoubtedly become one of the nation's most serious social problems. But when you get down to the facts of these cases, you usually find that the provocation was miniscule and that the child was acting in utter innocence. An irritable parent simply took his or her frustrations out on the little one over what proves to have been a piddling, insignificant incident.

Husbands and wives are on the verge of breaking up — over what? Some trifling thing that could be settled in an hour if the pair would have talked things out like adults. In fact, most marital problems have their genesis in trivia — petty things.

Christians often lose out on God's best because of giving in to petty little wants and desires. Remember those gold wire pins worn by so many people a few years ago? Just three letters: JOY. When asked the meaning, the wearer would recite, "Jesus first, Others next, Yourself last." Yes, that *is* a sure-fire formula for joy — but how many follow it?

A father sent his three children off to bed for quarreling over some trifling matter. They went, complaining over their grievances and the parental cruelty. But shortly after midnight, a fierce storm struck. At the height of the storm their father heard the shuffling of feet upstairs. Entering, he saw the children's empty beds and called out, "Where are you?" A tremulous little voice answered, "We're in the closet forgiving each other!"

What a great lesson for those of us who are often children with adult bodies!

I write unto you, little children, because your sins are forgiven you for his name's sake. 1 John 2:12

A wife stands facing her husband. He's been hitting the booze trail, and finding it too expensive for his legitimate income, he's been dealing in stolen goods on the side. The police have moved in, and he's now behind bars.

The man is broken and repentant, but he reasons that there's no way for his wife to have a shred of love left for him. Then, unexpectedly, she reaches through the bars, takes his hand in hers, and says through her tears, "Don't worry, honey. Everything's going to be all right!"

This illustration speaks to me of the promise God makes to those of us who fight the battle of life with so many human limitations and disabilities. So often, in my darkest hours of despair and seeming helplessness, I have felt His hand on mine and I've heard with the ears of my heart those wonderful words of solace and hope: "Everything's going to be all right."

The worst thing in the world is unforgiven sin. How vividly I remember the joy that flooded my being when I realized that God had forgiven all my sordid past with its many sins against Him. True, my parents had often forgiven me, but this had brought only a temporary "good feeling." When God forgave me, it brought a guarantee of everlasting life, for none can enter His presence without forgiveness.

If we confess our sins, he is faithful and just to forgive us our sins, and to cleanse us from all unrighteousness. 1 John 1:9

A happy heart makes the face cheerful, but heartache crushes the spirit. Proverbs 15:13 NIV

There is absolutely no question in my mind about whether or not we were made to laugh. Laughter is not only a tonic—it is a personality improver. Who ever heard of a popular sourpuss? Laugh wrinkles are attractive on any face and jolly people are usually remembered more fondly than those who take too grim an outlook on life.

Laughter, like any other gift, can, of course, be perverted, and sick humor is becoming increasingly prevalent. This is a great gift misused. Here is Paul's warning to the Ephesians: "But among you there must not be even a hint of sexual immorality, or any kind of impurity . . . because these are improper for God's holy people. Nor should there be obscenity, foolish talk or coarse joking, which are out of place . . ." Ephesians 5:3, 4 NIV.

Wholesome laughter, however, is a gift of God, and we have glimpses in the Bible of great joy in heaven. Revelation 19:9 speaks of the marriage supper with Christ, certainly a happy occasion.

Laughter in heaven? Yes, because of victory over earth's handicaps. Aren't *winners* always happy?

This is a vale of tears, and we are all part of it. But our sorrows are only temporary. Remember the words of our Lord to His disciples: "Blessed are you who weep now, *for you shall laugh*" Luke 6:21.

And they shall be mine, saith the Lord of hosts, in that day when I make up my jewels. Malachi 3:17

Throughout recorded history, man has had a fascination with precious gems. Jewels have influenced the course of history. And because the Bible calls us His jewels, it isn't difficult to understand why Satan has tried so hard to crush Christians throughout the years.

Genuine jewels can be distinguished from the fakes by their hardness. In 2 Timothy 2:3, Paul said, "Thou therefore endure *hardness* as a good soldier of Jesus Christ," and the early believers knew what that meant. Many of them were given the choice of denouncing their faith, or pitting their strength against hungry lions in the arenas or being burned at the stake. But they demonstrated their authenticity before the world.

In recent times, multiplied thousands in Russia, China, South America, and other areas of the world have proved to their tormenters that they were genuine jewels — not just glass beads!

Just what is a diamond? It is carbon, crystallized under great pressure and high temperature. And that's how God makes great Christians. He takes us into His laboratory of Grace, and through the chemistry of His Son's blood He processes us until we emerge as jewels — cut, buffed, and polished, and ready for Heaven.

It's a unique and wonderful experience and it can be yours when you really want it!

He is our peace, who has made us both one, and has broken down the dividing wall of hostility. Ephesians 2:14 RSV

A Christian woman wanted above all else to be a teacher, but as she neared graduation, her supervisor told her she had neither the personality nor aptitude for that role. Even her student teaching, she was told, was unsatisfactory, and she was advised to find something else to do.

But teaching was all she had ever dreamed of doing, and she called on God to help and guide her. Finally an opportunity came for her to teach "special" children in downtown New York. These pupils included every type—the shy, the withdrawn, the aggressive, the defiant. Finding that punishing or yelling at them was to no avail, she just loved them, and their response was amazing!

She now has more than fifteen years' experience with these kinds of students and here are some of her own comments:

Only the knowledge that Christ has this kind of love for me and everyone else has made it possible for me to have it, too. I have watched this way of love change children. I know I have come upon something so powerful and so redemptive that it defies description. Nothing can stand in the face of God's love, and nothing can stop it. It cuts through every defense mechanism, every fear and resentment. This way of love . . . cannot be bought or earned with great deeds. It cannot be learned in a college course. It comes quickest to the one who stands the lowest. It is a way of living that I am eternally grateful I have found.

Nothing ever happens *through* us until something happens *to* us—a genuine love for Christ.

15 REJOICING IN SUFFERING

If we suffer, we shall also reign with him. 2 Timothy 2:12

Many a person who literally worships physical culture, who eats all the right foods, jogs several miles a day, swims and plays golf and tennis, never gives a passing thought to the welfare of his inner being. Even though he has full control of his muscles and reflexes, his thoughts run wildly out of control, and he knows a great deal about mental suffering.

Because the body reacts to sensory experience, we are prone to think of our physical ailments as most serious. This, of course, is because our bodies are the tangible part of us; yet God is more greatly concerned with our inner selves than He is with our earthly shell.

"When I am weak, then I am strong," said Paul in 2 Corinthians 12. Rather than whining about his sufferings, he actually took pleasure in infirmities, insults, hardships, persecutions, and difficulties. Why? Because only through adversity and suffering could Paul show others the unique power that resides in the gospel with its total provision for man's every need.

Yes, Jesus Christ is adequate. He is with us in sickness and in health; in poverty or affluence; in danger or in safety; in shadow or sunshine. For the Christian, suffering is but a sometimes unpleasant prelude to an eternity in which suffering, in all its forms, will be unknown.

Believing this, we can see a divine purpose in suffering. Therefore the Christian can actually rejoice in it!

And though I give my body to be burned, and have not love, it profiteth me nothing. 1 Corinthians 13:3

In one of New York City's older residential areas, there was a fashionable church. The members were making a special drive to secure new members for the Sunday school, and children playing near the church were systematically approached by teachers seeking to build attendance.

Every Sunday morning, about fifteen or twenty minutes before the Sunday school hour, a boy of nine or ten years of age walked past the church. He was dressed in worn, but clean, clothing and the recruiters knew where he was going, for they had sent out scouts to track him. He was attending a small storefront church in a rundown neighborhood.

One of the more enthusiastic recruiters for the fashionable church stopped the little fellow one Sunday morning as he walked past on his way to the little storefront church. "Look, son," he said, "we've noticed that you're attending another Sunday school and I'm sure you would enjoy our classes and teachers. Why do you go that extra distance every Sunday when our church is so much closer?"

Squaring his shoulders and looking his interrogator straight in the eye, the boy said, as he prepared to continue his sojourn: "Why do I go to that other church? *Because they love a fellow down there!*"

My fellow believer, may the words of this nameless boy burn their way into our hearts this day, causing us to take inventory of our lives. May we ponder anew the words of our Lord, "This is my *commandment,* that ye love . . . as I have loved you" John 15:12.

Behold, I go forward, but he is not there; and backward, but I cannot perceive him: on the left hand, where he doth work, but I cannot behold him: he hideth himself on the right hand, that I cannot see him. . . . Job 23:8, 9

Job was in a dark tunnel. The light had gone out and he was groping to find someone. He edged backward—*nothing*. His hands went out to the left—*no one there*. To the right; still *nothing*. At such times the isolation of the soul seems absolute and God is nowhere to be found.

But more devastating by far is *not* groping for God in the tunnel of emergency. It is better to feel your need, and imagine Him as hiding from you, than to feel no need of Him at all. You see, nothing is more tragic than learning to live comfortably with *emptiness*.

When you look at your own life, is there anything suggestive of a pattern? Or do you say, with Job, "I cannot perceive Him . . ."? If so, look at Job's life. He knew adversity in a measure few will ever know; yet listen to what he added after voicing his complaint: "He knoweth the way that I take: when he hath tried me, I shall come forth as gold."

Faith finds its own answers to its problems. He knoweth the way that *you* take, my friend. Will you believe that? The future is already lit by His presence, and if you look back with honesty, you will admit that the way behind you is also marked by His presence.

There was a time when God hid Himself from His own Son. Jesus cried, "My God, my God, why hast thou forsaken me?" But that was only the man crying out in agony, for Jesus knew why the Father had forsaken Him. It had all been agreed upon before the foundation of the world. In this supreme event of all history, God showed where He was to be found.

In Christ, God comes out of hiding!

Without faith it is impossible to please God, because anyone who comes to him must believe that he exists and that he rewards those who earnestly seek him. Hebrews 11:6 NIV

The Bible wasn't written to prove God but to explain Him and to acquaint man with His attributes. However, faith must begin with belief in God, for He is the gateway to all spiritual understanding and experience. Before we can please God, we must believe He exists. That's clear enough, isn't it?

While belief in God is basic, it doesn't constitute, in itself, a ticket to heaven. I like this in-depth definition of biblical faith in the *Wycliffe Bible Encyclopedia:*

The Bible stresses that man as a creature was especially made for knowledge of his Creator, who reveals Himself to man in nature, in conscience, and, moreover, in particular historical events. This divine disclosure, climaxed in Jesus Christ as God's self-revelation in flesh, is authoritatively narrated and interpreted by the Scriptures.

But there is more. One must also believe that He is the Creator and Sustainer of all things, for the God we worship must be able to do that which man cannot do. And we must have a Person who loves us — not because we deserve His love, but because we are products of His creative genius.

All through the centuries of human alienation, God's love prevailed, but it took His appearance in human form to pay the ultimate sacrifice required to bear away the sins of the world. "Herein is love, not that we loved God, but that he loved us, and sent his Son to be the propitiation for our sins" 1 John 4:10.

So there you have Him — our God! Creator and loving heavenly Father to all who choose to join His family by faith, but an avenging judge to those who spurn Him.

So then they that are in the flesh cannot please God. Romans 8:8

A study of the New Testament will reveal that Jesus' disciples were perpetually hampered by opposing groups. Paul spoke on one occasion of "many adversaries," (1 Corinthians 16:9) and when he first entered the cities of the Greek mainland, he and his workers were surrounded by the uncomprehending and contemptuous.

Jesus repeatedly warned His followers of coming opposition, and the early Christians were prepared for it. They understood that the only effective way to adapt to a minority status was by means of an inner toughness. Peter wrote, "You must therefore be like men stripped for action" 1 Peter 1:13 NEB.

A dedicated Christian in any generation must understand that he belongs to a very minute segment of society — and always will. No believer can be fully prepared for the inevitable struggle until he or she appreciates the essential opposition there is to New Testament Christianity. Anyone who thinks differently is in for a surprise.

I am aware that if we are to successfully introduce modern people to Jesus Christ, we must make ourselves understood, and that involves a careful choice of our terminology. But God forbid that we would make the lines fuzzy in the hope of conjuring up something universally "acceptable." The gospel will never be attractive to the masses; the Christian faith will always involve a contrastive value system.

As a matter of fact, the strength of the Christian gospel lies in its dissimilarity, and the church's gravest danger is not the onslaughts of atheism, or even the undermining by the so-called New Paganism. The great peril lies in an unwillingness to oppose the modern mentality.

Robert Raines said it best: "The Church is meant to be at tension with the customs and traditions of every culture." Lacking this tension, we wind up with an impotent church, and there is nothing more pathetic than a church that tries to win a popularity contest!"

There is a way which seems right to a man, but its end is the way of death. Proverbs 14:12 NASB

To study carefully, and with preconception, the gospel and the epistles is to come to the unqualified conclusion that good works, although important, cannot save. If they could, God would not have sent His Son to the cross to die for us. He would simply have put man on probation and judged him at the end of his life by weighing his good deeds against his bad ones. But man was given every conceivable opportunity to save himself by his good works and he has failed, century after century after century.

So God sent Jesus to be every man's perfection for those who trust Him as Savior. This is the righteousness which Paul told the Roman church "is by faith in Jesus Christ, unto all . . . them that believe" (3:22).

Now that you have been introduced to what Jesus said about believing in His finished work, what is *your* decision? You must decide, you know. You either believe what He said, or you reject it.

Are you willing to take a chance on rejecting, even though you know that if you are wrong, you'll inherit a bleak, friendless, Christless eternity?

But God has given you and me an option. Jesus said, quite clearly and emphatically, that there is but one way to heaven, and that is through faith in Him. He said His Father gave Him to the world, in love, "that whosoever believeth in him should not perish, but have everlasting life" (John 3:16). Now you must either believe that, or disbelieve it. You must either choose this way, or some other way.

If you choose Christ and He delivers on His promises, you have gained everything. If you choose Him and He fails you, you still haven't lost anything. If however, you reject Him, and lose, you've lost everything — for all time!

I would be a very happy man if I could persuade someone reading these words to accept that challenge.

Whatever your hand finds to do, do it with all your might. . . .
Ecclesiastes 9:10

If anything good can be said about the Great Depression, it is that it
didn't accommodate the lazy. People either worked hard or went
hungry. I'm glad for those years because they taught me hard work.

This is not to imply, of course, that the harder one works in the
service of Christ, the more spectacular will be the outward results.
Alexander Cruden was a Scottish book-seller in London who died in
1770 at the age of sixty-nine. His name seldom appears in the roster of
great Christians, yet thousands of ministers and Christian laypeople
have depended on *Cruden's Concordance* which he published at the
age of thirty-six. Cruden exemplified the virtue of diligence.

Today, that virtue is practically non-existent in the lives of many of
God's people. The philosophy of "get what you can with as little
effort as possible" has unfortunately invaded the ranks of Christian
circles.

The Danish philosopher and theologian Soren Kierkegaard once told
a fable about a flock of geese that was flying south for the winter. One
gander, thinking himself wiser than the rest, decided to leave his
companions and settle down in a barnyard where several chickens
were gorging themselves on corn. He arbitrarily shared their fare.

Because it was so much nicer than flying, the great bird decided to
spend the winter there, but when spring came he heard his fellow
geese overhead and he stretched his wings to take flight. Alas, he
couldn't get off the ground! He had become so fat on the farmer's corn
that he was unable to perform his goosely function.

How like some who elect to take the way of least resistance. God
made us to *soar* — but many choose the barnyard, where we become
lazy and indolent, finally losing the ability to use the talents with which
we were originally endowed.

I urge, then, first of all, that requests, prayers, intercession and thanksgiving be made for everyone—for kings, and all those in authority. . . . This is good, and pleases God our Savior. . . .
1 Timothy 2:1, 2 NIV

Since many of those holding positions of authority in various realms of administration are neither professing nor practicing Christians, the question arises about whether Christians should pray for these men or women, or should they be challenged and, if possible, unseated?

Here we have a definite command: yes! It doesn't say to pray for those in authority only if they belong to our particular party or if they are totally honest. (I believe we criticize our elected officials over much and pray for them too little. Many are doing their best under chaotic conditions. God knows they need resources beyond their own upon which to draw.)

In Paul's day there were Christians in Caesar's household — servants of the Emperor (Philippians 4:22). Remember, Rome at that time was a city of want and waste and senseless cruelty. Shortly after Paul wrote to the believers in Philippi, Nero was to brand all Christians criminals and martyr thousands of them for their faith.

I believe this is why Christians are called upon to pray for those in authority — not always for personal victory, but that God's will may be done. There are times when God miraculously spares His people, but often Christians suffer under oppressive governments — in this life only, of course.

So we pray, not that God will necessarily spare us, but that He will work out His eternal plans for the nations, and that we will live out our faith even in an alien environment.

Why dost thou stand afar off, O Lord? Why hidest thou thyself in times of trouble? Psalm 10:1

It is an awful thing to doubt God, not only because it indicates mental, moral, and spiritual blindness, but because of what it does to the doubter.

"Now we see through a glass, darkly;" Paul told the believers at Corinth, "but then face to face: now I know in part; but then shall I know even as also I am known" (13:12). When the time is ripe, God will become visible, but it will be a day of glory only for those who have previously known Him by *faith*.

I see great mercy in God's "hiddenness." T. S. Eliot said that humans can't bear too much reality; perhaps this is true. Likewise, those who can't bear His written Word will never be able to look upon His presence *then*.

Mankind has a history of looking for God in the wrong places. God came in the person of Jesus Christ, and man stood beneath His cross and mocked, "If you're the Son of God, come down!" Because humankind refused to consider a merciful God, suffering and dying in the place of a sinful race, they looked past Him and missed him altogether!

Where is God? His presence fills the earth, air and space; but if you want to "see" Him, look at Jesus, who told His disciples, "He who has seen Me has seen the Father" John 14:9.

Jehovah, speaking through the prophet Jeremiah, laid out the conditions clearly. "Ye shall seek me and find me, when ye shall search for me with all your heart" (29:13).

I give eternal life to them; and they shall never perish, and no one shall snatch them out of my hand. John 10:28

The husband of a good friend died as the result of an accident, and she has been overcome with grief ever since. She now fears she isn't a Christian and that she won't meet him in heaven, and her letters are pathetically morbid. When she lost her assurance, she lost her joy and the strength God longs to provide in her loss. Gone is her "foretaste of glory divine." She has failed to trust God for His *keeping* power, as well as His *saving* power.

Notice Paul's triumphant words in 2 Corinthians 5:8: "We are confident, I say, and willing rather to be absent from the body, and to be present with the Lord." He is saying that we Christians have the assurance that when the believer's spirit leaves the body at death, he will be present with the Lord. *Period.*

Paul doesn't say, "I'm sure I'll be able to hold out faithful to the end"; he says, "I know whom I have believed, and am convinced [assured] that *He* is able to guard what I have entrusted to him for that day" 2 Timothy 1:12 NIV. If words have any meaning, that puts the responsibility on Jesus Christ, for none of us could ever in a thousand years be good enough to merit what He has prepared for those who have accepted Him and who serve Him.

My Christian friend, is it presumptuous for us to say we *know* we are going to heaven? Isn't it evidence of distrust when we indicate we "hope" to make it if we're lucky?

Jesus said, "He who believes in the Son *has* eternal life." How can that be less than forever?

Choose you this day whom ye will serve. Joshua 24:15

Every student of American history is familiar with the life of Aaron
Burr, who, through a strange turn of events, became Vice President of
the United States under Thomas Jefferson from 1801 to 1805. He was
later to be tried for treason—planning military action against the
United States government. The last years of his life were lived in
relative anonymity and disgrace.

Less well known, however, is the fact that Aaron Burr was a grandson
of the famous Puritan clergyman Jonathan Edwards. Vacillating
during his college years between studying law and entering the
ministry, he chose law.

There is a sidelight to the story. It is said that one day his
granddaughter, who had been converted to Christ, asked him why he
had never become a Christian. Burr is reported to have replied:
"When I was fifteen I attended a gospel service, but left without
making a decision for Christ. Once outside the church, I looked up and
said, 'God, if You won't bother me any more, I'll not bother You.' "
What a fatal choice!

Yes, *choice*, not *chance*, determines destiny. How many of our
daily decisions are made on the basis of personal pleasure and
convenience or of what others will think of us. God asks us to make
our choices in accordance with what He thinks . . . and commands.

That's why, in the long run, one's spiritual destiny is sealed, not by
God, but by a personal decision I call the *gift* of choice.

And the Lord said unto Cain, Where is Abel thy brother? And he said, I know not: Am I my brother's keeper? Genesis 4:9

There are many things for which I am not responsible. I share no blame for the years of bloodshed in northern Ireland or the Middle East. Neither have I contributed to the crimes that beset our nation. I have often raised my voice in protest of the moral toboggan upon which our nation has embarked, so I don't expect this generation's blood to be on my hands when I stand before the Great Judge.

On the other hand, there are situations and people for whom I *am* responsible in the area of the *rules* by which I have lived, the *example* I have set and the kind of *love* I have demonstrated.

Am I my brother's keeper? The answer is *yes* . . . and *no*. Yes, if we are talking about precept and example; no, if we mean responsibility for the final product. The men who, with great pains and at tremendous cost in labor and material, assemble the famed Rolls Royce automobile, are responsible for the product that leaves the assembly line — not for the mass of twisted metal produced by a drunken driver.

In much the same way, you and I are responsible for our conduct and standards we set and keep. In this sense, we are indeed our brothers' "keeper" — and the term *brothers* extends to mean sons, daughters, grandchildren — yes, even great-great-grandchildren.

What a privilege! Someone was right on target when he said, "Parents are just baby-sitters for God!"

And the peace of God, which transcends all understanding, will guard your hearts and minds in Christ Jesus. Philippians 4:7 NIV

An unusual woman was being interviewed by a reporter. Although a widow of many years, she had raised six children of her own and had adopted another twelve! Despite all the work and responsibility, she was a poised and charming lady.

"How do you manage?" asked the reporter.

"Well," she replied, "I'm in sort of a partnership."

"What kind?"

"A long time ago," she replied, "I said to the Lord, 'Lord, I'll do the work and You do the worrying.' I haven't had a worry since!"

What a beautiful Partnership.

When the late Peter Marshall was chaplain of the U. S. Senate, he once shocked that legislative body by opening a session with this prayer: "Help us do our very best this day and be content with today's troubles, so that we will not borrow the troubles of tomorrow. Save us from the sin of worrying, lest stomach ulcers be the badge of our lack of faith. Amen."

Incidentally, the word *worry* doesn't appear in the King James Version, but rather the word *careful,* which in the Greek means to become distracted. So Paul was really saying, "Don't worry about anything; just pray, and with thanksgiving present your request to God."

He will supply the peace if you meet the conditions.

To depart and be with Christ . . . is far better. Philippians 1:23

Actually, I am not an avid obituary fan, but when I occasionally read that column in the newspaper, I always find myself wondering how many of those whose names appear there died triumphantly? According to the accounts, many held impressive positions in certain lodges. Most were at least remotely associated with some religious sect or denomination.

But how many passed on with a valid Christian hope?

So few funerals these days contain the Christian note of triumph. Over the earthly remains of so few can be said, in complete honesty, "O death, where is thy sting? O grave, where is thy victory?" 1 Corinthians 15:55.

Dwight L. Moody once told an audience: "I have heard many tell of the *dark* valley of death, but the word 'dark' doesn't appear in the 23rd Psalm. It says, 'Though I walk through the valley of the *shadow* of death.' Did you ever see a shadow in the dark? All death can do is to throw a shadow, because Christ, the Light, is present. *We have nothing to fear!*"

Afraid? Of what?
To feel the spirit's glad release?
To pass from pain to perfect peace?
The strife and strain of life to cease?
Afraid — of that?

— E. H. Hamilton

. . . but be of good cheer; I have overcome the world. John 16:33

If we allow ourselves to bend or break under the weight of trouble, it means we have ignored or disobeyed this command. Jesus is saying we are to be of good cheer, even in times of personal trouble, national trouble, worldwide trouble. Another translation of the term "good cheer" appears in the New American Standard Version as "take courage," and how can we do that without being optimistic? Otherwise, we will succumb to pessimism — which is lack of trust — which is sin.

But just why should Christians be optimistic? Many are ill, some terminally. Many are poor. Others have been victims of natural disasters — floods, earthquakes, tornadoes, fires. But the Christian has the watch-care of the great God of heaven and the promise of Romans 8:28: "And we know that all things work together for good to those who love God, to those who are called according to his purpose."

All things *work together* for whose good? Ours! That is the foundation upon which we rest our perpetual optimism. God is our Father, and that means He is always looking out for our best interests.

Does God want — does He require — an ever-optimistic attitude toward life? I believe He does. Why else would He have said to His disciples, *"In the world you shall have tribulation;* but be of good cheer; I have overcome the world."

But I say unto you which hear, love your enemies, do good to them which hate you. Bless them that curse you, and pray for them which despitefully use you. Luke 6:27, 28

Christianity was born in an era of intense animosity between classes, races, and religious factions. The Samaritans and Jews hated one another, Rome barely tolerated the Hebrews, and there were factions between the Jews themselves. The peoples of Palestine were characterized by political rivalry, stealing, lying, and intrigue of every kind. Even love between marriage partners was rare, as most weddings were arbitrarily arranged before children reached physical maturity. And it was in this setting that Jesus introduced His message of love.

In the Greek language, love has three shades of meaning. On a strictly physical level, the word is *eros* (compare with our English word erotic) and obviously Jesus did not use this word when He told His hearers to love each other . . . and even their enemies!

The Greek word *phileo* describes love on a higher level — an affection for those who like us, and for the things we like. This is the kind of "love" that puts millions of marriages on the rocks every year as differences arise between partners.

But Jesus used the word *agape* — the giving, spending, and sacrificing love described in 1 Corinthians 13. I suggest that you read that beautiful chapter some time today and let its probing words challenge your heart anew. Then ask God to help you manifest agape love to others — even to those who may hate you in return.

And the world passeth away, and the lust thereof: but he that doeth the will of God abideth forever. 1 John 2:17

Prayer is a preparatory exercise in obedience — not an answering service. In seeking God's will, *my* will must be neutralized. I must have no objection to the answer God has for me. Prayer, then, prepares the way for submission to whatever His revealed will for me may be.

Prayer accomplishes something else. It cleanses me from sin in order that God can reveal Himself and His will to me. "If we confess our sins, he is faithful and just to forgive us our sins and to cleanse us from all unrighteousness" (1 John 1:9). Through confession I become able to understand the ways of God and to walk in them.

Prayer, however, will not — does not — manipulate God, causing Him to change His mind or say *yes* when the answer should be *no*. We parents may give in to our childrens' demands, but not God.

The length of my prayers has nothing to do with His answer, but it may have a lot to do with my own attitude. God doesn't give Brownie points for marathon praying, however.

Hysterical praying is also ineffective, as a general rule. I've learned not to make important decisions while distraught or mentally depressed.

Finally, if the will of God is important to me — and it should be — it isn't necessarily easy. It calls for dedication of mind, strength, emotions, and all of life's circumstances to Him.

O blessed, hallowed will of God,
To it I bow with heart devout;
I will abide in all God's will.
His way is best, I do not doubt.

The entrance of thy words giveth light; it giveth understanding to the simple. Psalm 119:130

Too often we are prone to arrange the circumstances so God won't have any trouble giving us *our way* as we seek His will for our lives.

It is well to remember that God isn't in a hurry, as we usually are, so don't put a time limit on His answer and don't assume He hasn't answered your prayer for guidance just because you don't have the evidence on Monday morning at ten minutes after eleven! "Tribulation worketh *patience,*" and if it takes waiting to perfect the virtue of patience in you, you are probably in God's will for the present, even if it's not exactly what you ordered.

Very few of God's revelations to me have been earthshaking. Instead, they have been revealed piece by piece over a period of time. I no longer have to have instructions concerning tomorrow, today. Reason and patience and submission usually take over . . . and the peace of God prevails.

George Müller, a man whose faith and answers to prayer were matched by very few in all of Christian history, once said:

I seek at the beginning to get my heart into such a state that it has no will of its own in regard to a given matter. Nine-tenths of the difficulties are overcome when my heart is ready to do God's will, whatever it be. When I am in this state, it is usually but a little way to the knowledge of what His will is.

That, my friend, is the testimony of one who found, and walked in, the will of God.

Let us consider one another to provoke unto love and to good works. Hebrews 10:24

The need to curb anger and exercise self-control goes beyond morality and spirituality. There are physical reasons as well. Dr. Walter Cannon, pioneer researcher in psychosomatic medicine at Harvard University, describes what happens when one loses self-control:

Respiration deepens; the heart beats more rapidly; the arterial pressure rises; the blood is shifted from the stomach and intestines to the heart, central nervous system, and the muscles; the processes of the alimentary canal cease; sugar is freed from the reserves in the liver; the spleen contracts and discharges its contents of concentrated corpuscles, and adrenalin is secreted.

But we are primarily interested in knowing how the Christian is to handle frustration and acquire self-control, and for the answer we must turn to The Book: "A soft answer turneth away wrath, but grievous words stir up anger" Proverbs 15:1. This tells us how to avoid a situation where self-control is threatened. In other words, don't let a situation of tenseness occur in the first place.

Next, keep life in perspective by maintaining a close, personal relationship with The Prince of Peace, Jesus Christ, striving to live in peace with the brethren and "endeavoring to keep the unity of the Spirit in the bond of peace" Ephesians 4:3.

Above all, remember that long-suffering is one of the fruits of the Holy Spirit that He longs to duplicate in our lives as believers.

For whoever would save his life will lose it; and whoever loses his life for my sake and the gospel's will save it. Mark 8:35 RSV

I get the impression that when people who are always trying to "find" themselves finally do, they are more confused than they were before! If I understand Jesus correctly, He urged people to "lose" themselves.

One of the special by-products of Christian conversion is deliverance from the illusion that we are supremely important. Actually, most of our trouble stems from putting ourselves first, instead of God. Small wonder the world is in such a turmoil. When man so elevates himself in his own eyes, it is like putting a five-year-old at the throttle of a high-speed diesel locomotive.

Jesus taught that as we exalt ourselves we diminish ourselves. "Whosoever shall exalt himself," He said, "shall be abased; and he that shall humble himself shall be exalted" Matthew 23:12. He was talking about "getting lost."

A minister once told of a home he visited in the hills of New Hampshire. At one time it had been a fine house, alive with activity and laughter. But as the years passed, the porch, with its frescoed columns, decayed. The outer rooms, unpainted and uncared for, one by one became uninhabitable. As the process of disintegration continued, the tenants keep retreating to the inner rooms, dragging bits of furniture with them, until they finally lived in just one room in the center of the rickety residence.

I have seen lives like that, haven't you? They just get emptier . . . emptier; smaller . . . smaller.

The title of a book in my library reads, *Try Giving Yourself Away.* You don't have to read it to get the message. Don't hoard your heart; don't spare yourself; don't be overprotective. Jesus said we gain by giving and we live by dying!

In these last days he has spoken to us by his Son. . . .
Hebrews 1:2

Any communication from God to man is of the utmost importance
and we do well to listen to what He is saying. It is not enough to lift our
eyes toward the vast umbrella of space, the mountains or the seas,
and expect them to deliver His message to us. You will never hear from
God merely by admiring His handiwork. That would be like trying to
become acquainted with a carpenter by examining a cabinet he has
built.

Then how can one hear from God? These words from the Bible (*The
Amplified Version*) lend clarity to the answer: "In many separate
revelations — each of which set forth a portion of the Truth — and in
different ways, God spoke of old to [our] forefathers in and by the
prophets. [But] in the last of these days He has spoken to us [in the
person of] a Son, Whom He appointed Heir and lawful Owner of all
things, also by and through Whom He created the worlds and the
reaches of space and the ages of time — [that is] He made, produced,
built, operated and arranged them in order" Hebrews 1:1, 2.

Through these verses we learn that God has spoken in a variety of
ways in the past, but that He is now speaking to mankind through a
Person — His very own Son. Jesus is "God in focus," the One we can
come to know personally, not as a historical figure alone. He is the
One who "carried the load of our sins in his own body when he died
on the cross, so that we can be finished with sin, and live a good life
from now on. For his wounds have healed ours" 1 Peter 2:24 TLB.

Communication must be a two-way street. Man must respond.

On several occasions I have met people who have twisted my
words to suit their own hostile purposes, and all attempts on my part to
untangle the distortion were futile. Attempting to resolve a matter that
another is determined shall not be settled is a bewildering experience.
Perhaps God is more familiar with this situation than we will ever be.
He seeks to communicate with human beings, but they will not listen.
He speaks through blessings, but they turn a deaf ear. He speaks
through misfortune, but is met by stony silence or profane utterances.

But God's voice is still heard by millions who have come to Him
through Christ. If you haven't heard it, could it be because you have
tuned Him out?

For we cannot but speak the things which we have seen and heard. Acts 4:20

No normal person lives on this planet without speaking. However restricted you may be in audible communication, you are telling the world something every day. You cannot remain silent, for you will deliver a message of some kind to every other human being with whom you come in contact.

I once lived in a city that housed the State School for the Deaf. I soon learned that the people I saw gesticulating with the fingers in a way most confusing to me, had a sign language that is an eloquent and sophisticated method of communication.

Yet there are husbands and wives, sons and daughters who cannot communicate with one another—not because of a language barrier, but because of opposite views and purposes. How tragic. Dialogue, if it exists at all, is like the grunting of two pigs instead of companionship between God-created individuals.

It is well for us to remind ourselves, also, that as we live our lives before others, we are constantly saying something to them—at our place of employment, in our own households, in the church. The question is, *what are we saying?*

Woodrow Wilson, the 28th president of the United States, told this story:

I was in a very plebeian place. I was in a barber shop, sitting in a chair, when I became aware that a personality had entered the room. He had come quietly in upon the same errand as myself, and sat in the chair next to me. Every word he uttered, though it was not in the least didactic, showed a personal interest in the man who was serving him; and before I got through with what was being done for me, I was aware that I had attended an evangelistic service, because Mr. Moody was in the next chair.

I purposely lingered in the room after he had left and noted the singular effect his visit had on the barbers in that shop. They talked in undertones. They did not know his name, but they knew that something had elevated their thoughts. And I felt that I had left as I should have left a place of worship.

What will your life be saying to others today?

. . . believing, you rejoice with joy unspeakable and full of glory.
1 Peter 1:8

A gloomy Christian is a contradiction in terms. I am reminded of
Bishop Charles Mead's young son who always sat in the front pew of
the church where his father preached. Above the arch over the pulpit
was a row of lights and the lad named each one for a book of the
Bible—Isaiah, Jeremiah, Lamentations, Ezekiel, etc.

One day after church, the little fellow seemed distressed. When
asked by his father what the trouble was, he replied, "Daddy,
Lamentations has gone out."

Good. Let Lamentations go out! We forfeit our Christian testimony
when we give way to depression. The Christian should be a joyous
person. When one is right with God the whole world is right. When
Christ is discovered as the Way, the Truth, and the Life, a joy springs
up in the heart that is unmatched by any other of life's many
experiences. When wrongs have been righted and broken
relationships mended, the result is analogous to the prodigal's return:
"They began to make merry." Things were right again, and joy has its
roots in rightness.

If our poor, tired world would only recapture that joy and sound
that note again, how quickly things would change. The early
Christians knew the power of the gospel to change lives, because
they had been changed. A new creative power had been released in
the world when Jesus rose from the dead, and this provided hope for
everyone. The doors of limitless possibilities had been thrown wide
open!

Eleven men with some good news changed the course of history!

The resurrection is not something that bears no relationship to this
age. Although it took place a long time ago, it still affects the lives of all
who believe. Something wonderful happens when people relate
themselves to the *rightness* revealed in Christ, the Lord of life.

Have you experienced this joyous faith in your own life? It's the
Christian's privilege. Don't miss it!

By faith . . . he [Moses] endured, as seeing him who is invisible.
Hebrews 11:27

As a minister, I am expected to know the reason for every human
predicament. This sometimes frustrates me, for I know how inept I am
in supplying answers. Given one wish, I would request what
Solomon asked: wisdom; but perhaps I know as much as God wants
me to know about many things.

The truth is that none of us knows all the answers relating to life
here and hereafter. God, in His wisdom, has left us with many blank
pages. As I look back over my life, however, I feel that God has given
me all the light I have needed, *as I have needed it*. I realize this
step-by-step policy frustrates many people; they want to know exactly
where they are now and where they will be tomorrow and the day
after. As Christians, they are piqued at God for demanding faith instead
of immediate answers.

My friend, you could read your Bible through fifty times a year and
never find precise reasons for every little detail of your life. If you
could, you wouldn't be living by faith — and faith is God's way. Read
again the imposing list in Hebrews 11 — all in God's *Hall of Fame*
because they believed when they couldn't see!

After many years of studying His divine Book, I can estimate with
fair accuracy what God expects of me . . . and what He doesn't. I don't
demand that my every trifling experience be validated with a
Scripture passage. Christians need to think and live within the
framework of the Bible as a whole, not in little bits and pieces.

Sometimes God reveals His purposes for us in detail as we pray and
commit ourselves to Him. At other times, we must simply accept His
love and sovereignty by faith, resting on the promise, "All things work
together for good to them that love God . . ." Romans 8:28. I agree
this is not always easy when there are clouds on the mountains and in
the valleys, but there is tremendous excitement and strength in
believing without seeing.

If any man be in Christ, he is a new creature [creation]: old
things are passed away; behold, all things are become new.
2 Corinthians 5:17

Dusty, a senior high school girl, confesses: "When I think of the
world, I get scared. It seems so restless. Morals are going down. People
don't seem to care much what happens any more. They are being
degraded!"

Dusty is a product of the TV age, a communication medium that
surrounds young people with the stimuli of their world, but doesn't tell
them how to react to it.

Is there an answer? Is something available that satisfies, that
provides meaningful goals more intriguing than a gasped-out life in a
polluted world, followed by oblivion?

Yes. It's an answer that has satisfied sincere people, young and old,
for two thousand years, and it is good in any society and in any kind of
a crisis. The Bible calls it being "in Christ," and it involves a number
of wonderful experiences.

First, there is forgiveness of the past: "The blood of Jesus Christ his
Son cleanses us from all sin" 1 John 1:7. What a song that puts in the
heart!

But it does more than take care of the past; it provides a joy-filled
present. How sad that the Christian life is often portrayed as a
negative, gloom-filled existence. That just isn't so! I've been around
Christians, young and old, for the better part of my life, and I tell you
unhesitatingly that they have more fun than anybody.

Well, just what constitutes a "good" time? I've come up with three
guidelines I'd like to share with you:

1. *A good time will not harm you physically, morally, or spiritually.*
2. *It will meet with the approval of decent society. It will be moral and
   it will be legal.*
3. *It will leave "a good taste" —no regrets.*

Listen . . . if you have to lie about where you were and what you
did; if you have to keep the shades drawn; if you have to speak in
whispers because what you are saying isn't fit for general
consumption, you didn't have a good time!

What time I am afraid, I will trust in thee. Psalm 56:3

The Christian who has never learned to take God's "No" with as much grace and resignation as His "Yes," will be barometrical in his spiritual life. God is not just the sugar and the cream: He is the whole cup. If we face this fact, it will keep us from vacillating between hot and cold, between loving God and being out of patience with Him.

I have never met a believer who has not encountered many days when God appears to be deaf, or on vacation. But how else could our faith be tested? If He never allowed us to lose, for a while, the sense of His presence, we would never learn to lean on His Word instead of our feelings. There comes a time when the swimming instructor must withdraw his supporting arms and make his pupil launch out on his own.

In much the same manner, God tones our spiritual muscles by making us walk strictly by faith. Faith is trusting when we cannot see or feel His presence. It is assuming He is near when every outward sign indicates He is far away.

But shadows are just as important to spiritual growth as sunshine — probably more so — for they are the agents through which our real mettle is tested. Actually, God never "withdraws" from us, but He does test us to determine whether our faith lies in emotional exuberance or in His promises.

It is a sign of spiritual retrogression when the Christian evaluates his or her relationship to God by material benefits. If God is real only when we have a secure job, good health, or when our children turn out well, then our association with Him is a frivolous, superficial thing and could end very quickly. God's best respresentatives are those who praise Him in the shadows, who rejoice when the cupboard is bare and when the body is sick; who can praise Him when coveted dreams go unfulfilled and when the news is unpleasant.

Any weakling can praise Him on the mountaintop. A genuine experience of faith reveals itself in the shadows!

So when you feel the urge to complain, remember those believers who kept a strong, sweet faith while wrestling with man-eating lions in the arena, when illuminating the Appian Way with their burning bodies, or when being pulled apart on the rack to amuse a sadistic emperor! Then, by the simple process of comparison, you may find your way to commitment and contentment.

If ye continue in my word, then are ye my disciples indeed.
John 8:31

Sooner or later, something we depend on will break down — an automobile, a vacuum sweeper, a toaster, a furnace. Fortunately, there are skilled repairmen in most areas who can be summoned, apprised of the problem, turned loose on it, then paid for their work.

There is an area of life, however, in which this simplistic ritual fails to work. Things break down within us and are not so easily repaired. While modern surgical science has learned to correct many organic problems and medical science can ameliorate minor ailments, there are mental, moral, and spiritual mixups that defy the best efforts of psychologists and other professionals. I receive letters every day from people whose problems are so complex and have been so many years in the making that they cannot be corrected by a paragraph in a letter or by a Scripture verse.

I am glad that today there are remedial processes to which people can turn when they experience failure and weakness — when tragedy strikes and when painful circumstances engulf them. But it requires spiritual knowledge that comes from daily familiarity with God's truth, plus the power of the Holy Spirit to implement in our lives the knowledge we possess.

I would never deceive anyone by saying that just because they are related to God through the spiritual birth, there will never be mechanical troubles along life's way. Often the closer we walk with Him, the more problems we seem to have. But there is divine purpose in all this. I believe God is saying, "Keep your hands off of this machine. I'll take care of it!" Maybe He will choose to slow us down with a heartache or a disturbing situation in the home. But remember, He knows where He wants us to go and we won't understand His plan until we get there.

Maybe you are in a turmoil today. The engine has sputtered and you think it's the end of the world. Why not stop fiddling with the carburetor and kicking the tires? Leave everything in the hands of the Master Mechanic who has a plan for you and who is never late.

Paul wrote his most joyous epistle when he had engine trouble and landed in a Roman prison. It was his letter to the church at Philippi, and seventeen times in those four short chapters he uses the words "joy" and "rejoice." He was talking about supreme confidence in the goodness and sovereignty of God.

Why become frantic when the Master Mechanic is near?

You cannot serve God and mammon. Matthew 6:24

Mammon is an Aramaic word meaning money, so what Jesus was saying in our text is that one cannot serve God and money at the same time. Notice, He didn't say one cannot *have* God and money, too. The word He used was *serve*.

Jesus had a lot to say about money — especially riches that ruled and contorted people. Then, as now, there were those who hoarded their riches and increased them by means of crushing usury and exploitation, while refusing to share the fruit of their labors with others less fortunate.

Did Jesus teach that money, per se, is evil? No, for without it, sustenance would be almost impossible. But money must never become one's master; it belongs to God, and we are to manage it for Him. The moment money becomes more to us than its use in the will of God, it is time to take inventory of its place in our value system.

Then why did Jesus say, "No man can serve two masters"? Because no one who puts God in His rightful place will allow money to rule his life. Conversely, one who worships money can *never* make Christ the Master of his heart.

A minister called on a wealthy businessman to ask for a contribution for the church. The man angrily retorted, "I wish I never had to hear another plea for money!"

"I won't ask you again, sir," the minister replied quietly, "but let me tell you a story. A year ago I had a precious little son. He always needed something — clothes, books, lunches. And there were doctor bills — big ones. At times I thought, 'If only I could get away from this asking for a while.'

"Sir, I did. He's gone now and I'll never hear him ask me for anything more. Death silenced his voice, his needs. Oh, I'd give anything to buy for him again."

Perhaps God's greatest punishment would be to remove *our opportunities to give.*

The Word was made flesh, and dwelt among us . . . John 1:14

How does an infinite God communicate with finite man? Only in human terms. A first-grade teacher communicates with her pupils in language first-graders understand, else a child in that class will learn nothing. Jesus came that God might speak to man in his own language and on his own level.

"The Word . . . dwelt among us." This is God expressing Himself to us in terms of human life—in precept and example we can understand. These, in fact, are the only terms we can comprehend. In Christ we see God in terms of a baby born in Bethlehem; in terms of a Man who lived a perfect human life and taught in simple parables all could understand; One who died on a cross, carrying the sins of the world, then rose again to prove that everything He had said and done was of God!

Now, if you were God and wanted to communicate to your creatures, could you choose a more simple, direct, eloquent way?

You say that a plan such as this is beneath God's dignity. But if we remember the keystone of Christ's life and teaching is that God *loves* us, we will understand that real love never stands on dignity. If you love someone and want to show it, you must discard all dignity. You run the risk of being laughed at, even spurned; but it is the only way you can discover whether your love brings a response.

This is what God chose to do at Calvary. And because He made us free moral agents, He expects a free response—not a forced one which would stifle the free response of requited love.

So God leaves to us the final decision of whether we will have Him in our lives. We have the option of believing the overwhelming evidences all around us, or closing our eyes to them. The only thing God will ever force man to do is stand trial for the way he has reacted to the evidence.

What has been *your* response to God's revelation of Himself through His Son?

Whosoever believeth that Jesus is the Christ is born of God.
1 John 5:1

John, the inspired apostle who wrote those words, lived with Jesus, leaned on His bosom, sat under His ministry for three years; if anyone knew what Jesus believed and taught, it was he. If John was "narrow," he got his narrowness from Jesus. He heard Him say, "I am the door: by me, if any man enter in, he shall be saved," and "He that . . . climbeth up some other way . . . is a thief and a robber" John 10:9, 1.

Fortunately, however, the gospel isn't narrow when it comes to admitting people into the family of God. The second birth is offered to all — Jews, Gentiles, Negroes, Anglos, Japanese — men and women, boys and girls, of every tribe and tongue and social level. In Christ, all become His children; there is no difference.

How I revel in that fact! As I have been invited to speak at gatherings across this nation, brethren of every race and class have come to hear me and shake my hand and tell me of their love for Christ. And I love them all, for they are my brothers and sisters, and between us is a deep and mutual love which is rooted in our common love for Jesus.

What draws us together in this strange and wonderful bond? A common Savior who died for all. What a wicked, unnecessary thing racism is! God made us all and the only difference between us is a thin pigment of skin or distinctive facial features. We are all citizens of the world Jesus loved and died for!

If you have never experienced this bond of brotherhood, you have a whole new experience awaiting you. There is a mystical bond between members of Christ's body and I can't explain it to you. You will have to experience it.

Recently I put my arm around a black brother who was a victim of multiple sclerosis. Our eyes were moist as we assured each other of our mutual prayers. To him I had always been Uncle John. There we were, a black fellow in his twenties and a white man nearing sixty — drawn together in the bonds of Calvary. For in Him, we *are* one.

So every one of us shall give account of himself to God.
Romans 14:12

American poet Ogden Nash once wrote this couplet:

Why did the Lord give us agility,
If not to escape responsibility?

This seems to reflect the mood of most moderns, but everything the
Bible teaches contravenes such a philosophy. Assuming a person has
the ability to make a personal decision, it follows that he or she has
the responsibility to make moral and spiritual decisions as well.

We must not blame others. Although I do not dismiss the problems
that can and do occur because of heredity and environment, I believe
that each of us has been given certain talents and boundaries of
responsibility by God. He has bestowed on each of us special gifts for
which we are responsible to Him to cultivate and use.

I sense an upsetting dearth of cultivated consciences among those
who profess to know and love Christ. It is my strong belief that we are
required to maintain an active and sensitive conscience before God at
all times in order to be everlastingly aware of what displeases Him. I
believe we should be familiar with Christ's "don'ts" as well as His
"do's," and that we should live in accordance with both.

Well, for what are we responsible? For one thing, we are responsible
for our treatment of others, for we are His representatives. We are also
responsible for our willingness to help those who are in spiritual and
physical need, and this reaches into the area of our personal
stewardship of time, our resources, and our priorities.

Daniel Webster, the great statesman, was asked, "Mr. Webster,
what is the most sobering, searching thought that ever entered your
mind?" Without hesitating, Webster replied, "My personal
accountability to God."

As it was with him, so may it be with us.

. . . brethren, whatsoever things are true, whatsoever things are honest, whatsoever things are just, whatsoever things are pure, whatsoever things are lovely, whatsoever things are of good report; if there be any virtue, and if there be any praise, think on these things. Philippians 4:8

Paul tells us in Romans 1 that God "gave them over to a reprobate mind . . ." (v. 28). This was not because He *made* them think evil thoughts. This they did themselves, because, as Paul explains, "they did not like to retain God in their knowledge," and for this reason they lost the ability to think and act decently.

There are many references in the Bible to our thoughts, minds, and will, and they usually convey the idea that we determine our destiny by our voluntary thought processes. Jesus spoke often about the power of the mind for good or evil and he said men will be judged by their words as well as their deeds. Both are predicated upon our thoughts.

Then what about the unsavory thoughts that occasionally cross the Christian's mind? I know this is a trite illustration, but we need to remind ourselves of it. "We cannot keep birds from flying over our heads, but we can keep them from nesting in our hair!" While none of us can go through life without temptations, we can, with God's help and the exercise of our God-given will power, keep temptation from lingering long enough to be converted into evil deeds.

Any normal person can control his thoughts, and therefore his actions. That we are capable of this is borne out in the Biblical requisite for conversion—believing. If people had no control over their thoughts, and consequently their decisions, belief as means of salvation would be a cruel mockery.

The mind, however, is never under true supervisory control until it is offered in complete surrender to God. Only as the natural *mind* is renounced for the mind of the Spirit, can we know how to direct our thoughts. Certain thought processes belong to those whose hearts belong to God and whose minds are under His control.

Paul admonished the Philippians thus: "Let this mind be in you, which was also in Christ Jesus" (2:5). Only when we have His mind, through faith, can we think His thoughts.

Keep your heart with all vigilance, for from it flow the springs of life. Proverbs 4:23 RSV

Boredom. What causes it? And why will people go to almost any lengths to avoid it?

The answer lies deep within the unreachable ranges of human emotion which the Bible lumps under one general term, the "heart." It is this indefinable core of human consciousness that the specialists are unable to touch with their drugs and knives and psychotherapy.

God made us to lay hold on *something* — to wrap ourselves around something — and with what or whom we are concerned determines whether we are bored or fulfilled. Bored people feel they have nothing to live for, nothing to do, outside of themselves. "Hollow men," T. S. Eliot called them. Boredom is self-imposed emptiness, the curse that life puts into a heart too lazy and too empty to face responsibility, and too fearful to give itself in love.

I am purposely avoiding the term "empty," for technically, nature won't tolerate a vacuum. There is no such thing as an empty glass; even when it contains nothing else, it is full of air. Nor is man ever totally empty. That was the point in Jesus' illustration in Matthew 12:43-45. One unclean spirit left, but he was soon replaced by seven others more wicked than himself. The human heart has innate hungers and affections that must be fed, and when this vacuum sets in, people turn to every imaginable substitute to fill it.

But why, you ask, would a God of love allow His creatures to have this insatiable appetite? Because boredom is part of His good news. It is proof of our higher heredity, and without this gnawing inner hunger we would never seek Him.

I talked not long ago with a young couple who, only a few months before, had received Jesus Christ as their personal Savior. They had been hitting the night spots, poking fun at Christianity, and wondering how those who called themselves Christians found "anything to do." They said, "We have had more to do since we came to know Christ (and have been happier doing it) than we ever dreamed possible less than a year ago."

Eternity in the heart! Here is the genuine alternate to boredom. No one has ever had his heart filled by the world but God has planted eternity in every heart, and herein is found escape from boredom.

Come ye apart . . . and rest awhile. Mark 6:31

I am concerned these days about how tension gets to God's people, for we cannot be at our best when we are exhausted or when our nerves are on edge. If I were the resourceful preacher I should be, I might be able to provide some sure-fire answers to the dilemma, but unfortunately I cannot.

I do know, however, that there were times when Jesus had to get away from the crowd to meditate, rest, and pray. He also advised His disciples to do the same. Having taken on a human body Himself, He knew they were subject to physical, mental, and emotional breakdowns, and he taught them to relax on occasion, even though they were busily engaged in His work.

Relaxing requires planning and determination, but it can be done. While most of us have neither the time nor the money to visit the world's health spas, perhaps we wouldn't enjoy them if we did. We must find ways to escape life's everyday tensions in the midst of our busyness. We owe it to ourselves, and to our God, if we are to be of use to Him and others.

The Psalmist knew this; that is why we have the Lord speaking through him in Psalm 46:10: "Be still, and know that I am God." We need periods of calm and reflectiveness — times when we find that quiet place with Him where our physical and spiritual "batteries" are recharged.

You see, God has arranged that each of us, His children, can take a tiny vacation every day. We need a respite from the grind where we can iron out the wrinkles of the mind and escape from the bustle of life. How? Through fellowship with God that is predicated on a personal knowledge of Christ, His Son.

So if you find yourself climbing the walls today because life has closed in on you, take the time to surmount the petty, and you can experience life as boundless as the love of God — as exciting as His eternal promises.

The late Mrs. Charles Cowman wrote: "If we sadly say to ourselves, 'There is no music in a rest,' let us not forget there is the *making of music* in it."

Out of the depths have I cried unto Thee. Psalm 130:1

According to an eminent doctor, the major killers are not heart disease, cancer, and accidents, but calendars, telephones, and clocks. People who worry about their jobs, their health, their security, and old age, often dip below the line of mental stability to where their emotions become a destructive power instead of the driving force of life.

The struggle with ethics is another cause of depression in today's society. Call it what you will, a guilt complex is very real. To violate what Paul calls "the law of God," is to become sick with the weight of unforgiven sin.

People should learn to ventilate their feelings of depression — tell their story. That's why prayer is so therapeutic. "Tell it to Jesus" is more than a song title; it is a mental and spiritual boon.

Let me recommend the most helpful therapy I have found for depression: dwelling on the power and greatness and goodness of God. "I am convinced," Dr. A. J. Hadfield once said, "that the Christian religion is one of the most potent influences we possess for producing that harmony, peace of mind, and confidence of soul which is needed to bring health and power to nervous patients."

So learn to dwell on God's love, His sovereignty, and His interest in you. We all need to know that Someone who can help us is truly concerned about every phase of our lives.

Finally, read the Bible. A famed psychiatrist said, "I dreamed of writing a handbook that would be simple, practical, easy to understand, and easy to follow. Then, quite by accident, I discovered that such a work had already been completed."

He was referring, of course, to the Bible which the Christian world has been holding in its hands for the last two thousand years.

For I was envious of the arrogant, when I saw the prosperity of the wicked . . . They are not in trouble as other men are; they are not stricken like other men. Psalm 73:3, 5 RSV

Poor David; we must admit he is realistic in his appraisal. Maddening incongruities *do* appear to exist, and he couldn't understand why the wicked often prosper and live to a ripe old age, while just as frequently the righteous are struck down in youth or middle age, victims of the most excruciating afflictions. Why are children born blind or crippled; why do tornadoes and earthquakes and avalanches devastate sleeping towns, killing or maiming God's children along with the most blatantly evil?

Well, in the search for an explanation, there are four principal attitudes open to us:

1. *We may despair of a solution and express our frustrations in bitter skepticism.*
2. *We may conclude that good and evil are a dualism about which nothing can be done one way or the other.*
3. *We may consider evil an illusion or an instrument of ultimate good.*
4. *We may stop trying to rationalize life's puzzles and throw the entire matter into the hands of a sovereign and loving God, believing that in His good time, He will grant us understanding.*

The first two presuppose fatalism. The third is, in substance, pantheism, that God is all and all is God. Evil is not real; it is an illusion of the material senses. (In this world, there is nothing more real than sin and pain and death.)

The fourth may at first appear to be an insult to intelligence. What possible good can be served through sickness, tragedy, death? To the secular person, the present is supremely important, so it is natural to censure God for permitting hardships to exist.

But I, for one, consider life's disciplines as being for my good, knowing that when my course is run, I will look back and know that God was loving and just in all His dealings with me and that life's pains and sorrows were necessary refining influences. In my judgment, that makes sense!

For now we see through a glass, darkly; but then face to face: now I know in part; but then shall I know even as also I am known. 1 Corinthians 13:12

It is fitting that the New Testament should end with the book of Revelation, for here John addressed the early Christians at a time when the Romans were trying, however unsuccessfully, to destroy Christianity. Things must have looked mighty grim to John as he began to record those Patmos visions, but by the time he had finished, it was becoming apparent that Rome and all her counterparts would fall, and that, in the end, a kingdom of righteousness would be set up on earth.

To believe Romans 8:28, therefore, is to believe that, despite all the seeming evidence to the contrary, history *does* have meaning, and that it is moving, however circuitously and unevenly, toward divine ends.

Most important of all, Romans 8:28 is working for our good as individuals. It tells us, that Christians don't carve out their own careers, but are divinely led into and through them.

"I did not devise my way," said Graham Taylor, a noted religious leader at the turn of the century; "I discerned it." The first message Morse sent over his newly invented telegraph system contained four words: "What hath *God* wrought?"

But while many of the same circumstances happen to us all, we don't all respond to them in the same manner, and that makes a difference in their outcome. What one considers a blessing, another may consider a tragedy. I have seen Christians praise the Lord in adversity, and I have known them to die triumphantly — all because they drew upon spiritual resources that made them brave, that enabled them to show the world that they, like Paul, could do all things through Christ.

Christian friend, whatever happens to your own private, individual world, even though it appears to be the worst possible misfortune, put your life into His capable hands. Then leave it there. Trust God, and give Him time. Right now He is working everything out for your good. You may not see it, but then, you're not supposed to because that would destroy the important element of faith.

Now through glass darkly — then face to face! God help us to grasp the message!

Let your light so shine before men, that they may see your good works, and glorify your Father which is in heaven. Matthew 5:16

Among the sea's many phenomena, the emission of light by living organisms is a standout. Known by the term *bioluminescence,* this phosphorescence is created by marine creatures of the deep, and any disturbance such as the breaking of waves on a ship's prow causes these tiny organisms to glow like the lights of a large city seen from the air at night. While individually each is smaller than the head of a pin, collectively they produce light that is sometimes bright enough to illuminate the pages of a newspaper.

Could this have been what Job alluded to when he spoke of a "leviathan leaving a shining track behind him" Job 41:31, 32?

An itinerant preacher stayed one night in a rural home. A lad, saying nothing, but listening intently, heard this good man say some things that made him want to be a Christian. The boy was T. DeWitt Talmage, one of the greatest orators and defenders of the faith of the nineteenth century! He made a path to shine after him.

Are you and I shining lights to those across whose path we travel? Are we shedding light, or contributing to the darkness? Remember, there are more people who are crying than laughing; more stomachs hungry than filled; more homes disturbed than tranquil. What are we doing about it? As each infinitesimal plankton shines its best, so we, in concert with many others, can leave a glowing path.

I have never had a desire to be famous. The responsibility is too great, the burden too heavy. But I do want the preacher who stands over my clay to be able to say in complete honesty, "This man wiped away some tears; he lifted some burdens; he drew some souls to the heart of the Savior. Ours is a little better world for his having passed through it."

I'll settle for that, knowing that although I was not the sun or the moon, I was at least a pinpoint of luminous plankton, helping to light the pathway of some storm-tossed voyager.

How about you?

If ye endure chastening, God dealeth with you as with sons; for what son is he whom the Father chasteneth not? Hebrews 12:7

A popular writer once said, "An experience is not a failure if through it we discover ourselves." We can learn valuable lessons from such experiences, ensuring that our failures have not been wasted.

When Nathaniel Hawthorne lost his position in the Custom House in Salem, Massachusetts, he went home and announced to his wife that he was a complete failure. To his amazement, she greeted the news with delight. "Now," she said, "you can write your book."

Phillips Brooks prepared himself for a teaching profession, but he failed in that so ingloriously he despaired of ever doing anything above mediocrity. Then God called him into the ministry, and he gained an international reputation as a preacher during his twenty-two-year ministry at Trinity Protestant Episcopal Church in Boston.

I have concluded that a lot of people are failures simply because they never "hit their stride." They have talents which, if used for God, would make them immortal. Unfortunately they make injudicious choices and end up as ciphers.

Perhaps today you are overcome with a sense of failure. You feel you are just marking time at the office, or in the shop. Perhaps you, as a mother, are tired of the same old grind, managing the children, running the household, cleaning a littered house. Listen; unless you live on a desert island, without a human contact, you have a ministry. If you belong to Jesus Christ, you have a message someone is literally dying to hear. I guarantee that if you make someone else happy, you'll be happy.

What if you have made mistakes, if life is "blah"? Get to the root of your failure — then rectify it. The prodigal son, after living riotously in the far country, "came to himself," realized he was living an empty, foolish life, and did the only sensible thing. *He went home!*

The president of the IBM Corporation is reported to have said to a discouraged young writer: "Every one of your rejected manuscripts was rejected for a reason. Have you pulled them to pieces looking for that reason?" He was really asking, "Have you put failure to work for you?"

But we are citizens of Heaven; we eagerly wait for the saviour who will come from Heaven, the Lord Jesus Christ. He will change these wretched bodies of ours so that they resemble his own glorious body, by the power of his which makes him in command of everything. Philippians 3:20, 21 Phillips

Some time ago, I lost one of the dearest and closest friends I have ever had. For me, it was an inexpressible loss; for him it was a glorious graduation. The tears I shed were for myself, not for him.

Those of us who loved him in the Lord will always remember him for his unwavering faith in Jesus Christ and his continual readiness to serve others. During our many years of friendship, we never talked about "pie in the sky." We talked about the needs of this old world and those about us. My friend devoted nearly two years of the closing days of his life to a criminal rehabilitation program that would have discouraged me the first day. He did something practical with his life, for the glory of Christ.

After his "graduation" into the presence of the Lord, person after person told me, through tears, that he was the best friend they had ever known. (Don't tell me that Christians ignore their social responsibilities. They not only know where they are going; they are anxious to do all they can for others along the way.)

One day I will see my friend again and we will renew our fellowship with one another in our new, glorified bodies. No cancer. No coronaries. No feebleness. No diabetes. No pain. No sorrow. No death!

What will heaven be like? The apostle John uses the imagery of earth's most precious metals and stones to describe its splendor, but towering above all its beauty is the description of life without pain, and tears (Revelation 21:4).

Over the casket of every child of God could be this caption: "Addressee has moved. Permanent address: c/o Jesus Christ, Heaven."

Life is forever!

But above all things, my brethren, swear not, neither by heaven, neither by the earth. . . . James 5:12

A little girl went to Sunday school for the first time in her life. The Christmas season was approaching and the teacher told the story of the Savior's birth, the subsequent visits by the shepherds and the wise men, and she added, "And they called his name 'Jesus.' "

A look of sheer horror came across the little girl's face. "Why," she asked in utter incredulity, "did they name such a sweet little baby a swear word?"

She had never heard the name of Jesus used in reverence!

Well, why do people swear? I believe it is chiefly because the mind, when ruffled by momentary excitement, seeks a safety valve. It seizes upon expressions used by others under emotional strain and soon swearing becomes an integral part of the vocabulary and a person forms the habit of swearing without being conscious of it.

Years ago a nobleman visited the famous Wedgwood pottery plant in England. A fifteen-year-old boy showed him around while Mr. Wedgwood himself followed a few steps behind. The peer, although a fetching conversationalist, was also a very irreverent man, and he captivated the lad with his profane statements until the boy was laughing heartily at everything he said.

Later the man visited with Mr. Wedgwood in his office. The latter took a beautiful piece of pottery which the nobleman wanted, and let it drop to the floor where it shattered into a thousand pieces. "Why did you do that?" the man demanded. Replied the pottery firm's owner: "There are things more precious than this piece of pottery. I can make another vase as beautiful as this, but you cannot give back to that boy the simple faith and reverence you destroyed with your sacrilegious talk."

Now the question: *How does one shake the habit?*

1. *Ask God to forgive you for that awful backlog of words you have uttered in the past, claiming His promise in 1 John 1:9.*
2. *Then cultivate a profound sense of reverence for the name of God. Remember Him as omnipotent, omnipresent, omniscient, righteous, and loving. Jesus taught His disciples to pray to the Father, "Hallowed by Thy name."*

Never think of Him in any lesser terms.

. . . now I know in part; but then shall I know even as also I am known. 1 Corinthians 13:12b

Man walks a very narrow path. He cannot go too high, for he was not made for excessive altitude without space gear. He dare not go too deep, for he is not able to endure great depths. Even his body temperature has rigid limits: he dies if it deviates more than ten degrees in either direction. Man dies of thirst and exposure on the desert; he freezes to death in the Arctic regions. His nervous system is so delicate that it is subject to very narrow limits. Too much strain, too much knowledge, and his fuses blow.

Knowing this, God has limited man's intake. This is mercy!

Someone has noted that man could not stand to hear all the sounds and see all the sights by which he is surrounded. There are sounds beyond the wavelength of our ears that would blow our minds if they were to burst upon our consciousness, just as there are colors so brilliant they must reach us in the form of sound waves, else we would be blinded by them. We live in an ocean of energy from which we are providentially protected, and were God to lower but one of these barriers, all life would perish from the face of the earth.

The little men who raise clenched fists to heaven and cry, "Show me your God!" are pathetic indeed. On the morning of July 16, 1945, near Alamogordo, New Mexico, scientists ignited a man-made candle atop a steel tower surrounded by delicate sensors designed to record theretofore unknown data. The switch was thrown, and the flash of light illuminated mountains ten miles away with the brightness of noonday. There was a sudden wave of heat, followed by a tremendous roar as the shockwave passed and echoed in the valley. The rising ball of fire, dissolving in a mushroom cloud, rose 400,000 feet in the air. There was no trace of the steel tower, but the desert sands were fused into glass for a radius of nearly 2400 feet.

Now, if that little bit of power from God's world could so shatter man and the works of his hands, where would he hide if God were to reveal Himself in all His majesty and essence? It is because of God's mercy that He remains hidden. If we cannot face a candle, how can we look at the sun?

One of the most mind-expanding verses in the Bible is found in Revelation 3:20: "Behold, I stand at the door and knock." The God who cannot reveal Himself to man in His essence because of His mighty power, can knock meekly at the door of man's heart and ask, "May I come in?"

What has your answer been?

He that is not with me is against me; and he that gathereth not with me scattereth abroad. Matthew 12:30

The teaching of the New Testament is that one is either *for* Jesus Christ or *against* Him. But this sacred verity has not prevented many from developing a sort of mongrel attitude of mind—a "third dimension," so to speak. It is assumed possible, by man, to simply decline to take either side, considering themselves "neutrals." Pilate did so by saying, "I never argue religion or politics," in so many words, placing himself in a kind of "demilitarized zone."

Should there not be some credit to so harmless an attitude? After all, didn't Pilate wash his hands before the crowd that day, thus showing that he shunned all responsibility in the fate of Jesus Christ? Didn't that clear him of guilt in the events that followed? No!

Many today have convinced themselves that they, like Pilate, are neither for nor against Christ. In fact, they are inclined to say flattering things about Him. They acknowledge His teachings as most instructive; they believe He was a wise and good Man. They might even be persuaded to holler, "Hurrah for Jesus!" if the occasion warranted it. But there is no place for Him in their lives. As for His redemptive work on the cross, this makes them a little hostile. They don't want to become too "involved" with Him.

But Christ is the Unavoidable Person. When the Apostle's Creed is recited in our churches, the reference to the Savior is followed by one to Pilate—"Suffered under Pontius Pilate." So you see, Pilate *did* make a decision—even though he tried so desperately to escape making it.

For the sake of absolute clarity, my friend, let me stress this point again; no man or nation can avoid Jesus Christ. If you have decided to wait, you have said *no!* I know this is blunt, but I must tell you the truth. I didn't make the rules; these are set, and immutable. Pilate took water, washed his hands and said, "I am innocent of the blood of this just person." But was he?

Speak to one another with psalms, hymns and spiritual songs.
Sing and make music in your heart to the Lord. . . .
Ephesians 5:19 NIV

Some of us have a hard time meeting that admonition, even in our
comfortable homes or driving along in our fine automobiles. But Paul
wrote those words from a dark, dank, squalid prison cell. His heart
could sing because he had an eternal hope upon which he had fixed
the eyes of his soul.

Oh, Christian friend, stop counting your sorrows and your so-called
"bad breaks," and start today to count your blessings. The devil
would like to steal your joy and your trust in God's promises, and if
you allow it, he will paint your life's picture so dark that you will
doubt whether you have any blessings to count.

Let me share an incident which will never fade from my memory:

Many years ago, it was my privilege to visit one of my listeners, an
old gentleman whose wife had gone before and who had spent
several years in a nursing home. His letters to me had always been
cheerful, and when I walked into his room I could scarcely believe
my eyes.

The man was so rigid with arthritis of the spine that he had to be
helped to move even an inch!

As I reached down and tenderly took his crippled hand in mine, he
looked up through tear-dimmed eyes and said, "Oh, brother Jess, I'm
so glad you came. I wanted to be able to tell you face to face what a
wonderful Saviour I have and how good He has been to me!"

I left his room that day a humbler man, ashamed of my trivial
complaints.

Treasures are found in the darkness,
And riches are hidden in store;
And sorrow oft gives us a song to sing,
Unknown to us heretofore.

A merry heart doeth good like a medicine: but a broken spirit drieth the bones. Proverbs 17:22

Does God have a sense of humor? Some find that question debatable, but I have good reasons for believing He does. Just look at some of the animals He made—many of them hilarious both in looks and actions. Someone has said, "Laughter is wholesome. God is not so dull as some people make out. Didn't He make the kitten chase its tail?"

Some people, however, laugh at the wrong things. I have always felt that a person diminishes himself or herself by laughing at a dirty joke. Not all laughter represents genuine joy, as I discovered many years ago, but a good laugh at no one else's expense is tonic for the soul.

Why did God give us the gift of laughter? I believe it was to keep life in balance, for we have all been born into a world replete with sorrow. But if you have the hope of heaven in your soul, knowing that when you get through this brief vale of tears there is everlasting joy awaiting you, you can be joyous with a purpose.

God doesn't want us to be giddy, but He does want us to be happy. There's a difference. A bishop known for his cheery disposition was asked the secret of his happiness. I think his answer is worthy of our attention:

First, I look up to heaven and remember that my principal business is to get there. Then I look down upon the earth and think about how small a place I shall occupy when I am dead and buried.

Then I look around and see the many who are so much worse off than I am, and it is then that I learn where true happiness lies, where all our cares end, and how little reason I have to complain.

My friend, God meant for us to be happy, whatever our lot here on earth. If your joy has run out, ask Him to replenish it today. A dour attitude dries the life like a searing wind, but a *merry* heart does good like a miracle drug.

. . . That the aged men be sober, grave, temperate, sound in faith, in charity, in patience. Titus 2:2

If you are as sensitive about your age as some people I know, you are probably telling me to mind my own business. But my reference is not to the number of years you have been on this planet, but to your maturity. By what criteria do you measure your success — your worth?

Many people are pleased with themselves because of the money they have made, the distant shores they have visited, or the academic heights to which they have risen. But can we gauge a person's moral maturity by cash or real estate, the extent of his travels or by degrees earned or conferred?

Some feel they have earned the right to success by taking life's distresses stoically and unbowed. But my question is not how stoic you may be, but how mature. Lack of concern over life's vicissitudes may not represent strength of character at all. It may represent irresponsibility.

Well, how old *are* you? Many a moral and spiritual infant drives an expensive car, lives in a luxurious home, and counts his holdings in six or seven figures. One's real worth is measured by what he does for others. Begin thinking about some fetter you can untie, some nakedness you can clothe, someone you can point to Christ. Oh, there is much to do if you are old enough to do it.

How old was Paul? Luther? Moody? One does not tabulate such giants in terms of years. What difference does age make in men such as these? Their influence has never died, nor will it!

Parents often say to their children, "Act your age," or, "I'll be so glad when you grow up." But how old will they be when they are grown if they follow in your footsteps? Many children are moral dwarfs because like begets like.

You may have been a spiritual runt for many years, but God is able to enrich and develop your life if you will allow Him to. He can redeem the ravished years and add new, exciting dimension to any yielded life. He has the necessary ingredients; you need only ask Him.

With my whole heart have I sought thee; O let me not wander
from thy commandments. David — Psalm 119:10

The Bible is not a book; it is sixty-six books. It is a literary miracle that
came into being without a human plan or any collective effort on the
part of its writers. Little by little, part by part, century after century, it
formed in fragments and unrelated portions. One man wrote part of it
in Syria, another a part in Arabia, another a part in Italy and Greece.

Usually a book is brought into being when someone decides to
write it. Then a plot is conceived, material collected, copy written or
dictated; it is edited and re-edited and finally published and distributed.
But always it is written by one or collaborating authors within their
generation.

The Bible, however, was fifteen hundred years in the writing, and
the events recorded in it cover sixty generations. Amid the strain and
haste of man, God's great Book grew — here a bit of history, there a
prophecy, a poem, a biography — until at last it emerges complete,
ready for the heart of mankind.

When Moses died there were only five portions of the Bible
completed. When David ascended the throne of Israel a few more
parchments were readied. Little by little the princes, priests, and
prophets placed on this mounting accumulation their contributions,
some great, some small, until the entire Book was completed as we
have it now, intact and complete. Josephus, the Jewish statesman,
soldier, and historian wrote in the 1st century B.C.:

*Never, although many ages have elapsed, has anyone dared to take
away or add to or transpose anything whatsoever, for it is implanted in
all Jews from their earliest childhood to speak of them as decrees or
statutes of God.*

To the Jewish mind the Old Testament has no rival. That the New
Testament should have been written by Jews is in itself a miracle!

Yes, the Bible is overwhelming proof, by the very manner of its
formation, that it is a divine proclamation.

Forever, O Lord, thy word is settled in heaven. Thy faithfulness is unto all generations. Psalm 119:89, 90

An amazing fact is that not a line of the New Testament was written until at least fifty years after Jesus was born. Then, without collaboration or unity of plan, the books began to take form. Without consultations, committee meetings, or prearrangements between Matthew, Mark, Luke and John, each wrote as directed by the Holy Spirit. There was no agreement that Matthew should write of Christ as King, that Mark should portray Him as the Worker, that Luke should show Him as Man, and John should depict Him as the Son of God. Yet that is the way the books came out, each presenting a different facet of the same Christ.

This is a fact that moved Bishop Westcott to write:

There is no trace of any designed connection between the separate books, and still less of any outward unity or completeness in the entire collection. If the books combined to form a complete whole, then this completeness is due, not to any conscious cooperation of the authors, but to the will of Him by whose power they wrote and wrought.

Not the least of the miracles claimed for the Bible is the fact that *it is here!* Remember, it is an old Book and what other can you name that was written a thousand years ago and is still read today?

Were the Bible an ordinary book, it would need to be translated, transfused, and adapted to each differing culture and clime. Oriental books (and the Bible is such) must be changed to appeal to the Western mind—but not the Bible. Whether taken to Greenland, or India, or Europe, or South America, it satisfies a universal longing. Only a book inspired by God Himself could be so adaptable.

The Bible, on the other hand, is the most widely-circulated Book in the world. Translated into more than 1,000 languages and dialects, it is, in many parts of the world today, a Book so sought after that many people would give a fortune for a copy if it were available and within their means. Who would dare call this "just another book"?

A converted African cannibal sat reading his Bible. A European trader asked him what he was reading. "The Bible," the native replied.

"That book is out of date in my country," observed the trader.

"You are fortunate it is not out of date here," replied the native, "for if it were, you would have been eaten long ago!"

Blessed be the God and Father of our Lord Jesus Christ, who according to His great mercy has caused us to be born again to a living hope through the resurrection of Jesus Christ from the dead. . . .1 Peter 1:3 NASB

The disciples based every argument for the Christian faith on the fact of the resurrection. If Jesus rose from the dead, everything they were saying about Him was true. If He didn't, the message they were preaching was dead religion, no better nor worse than thousands of others that vie for men's attention and devotion.

While there is no way to get an instant replay of the Resurrection, yet there is ample corroborative proof for anyone who earnestly and honestly seeks it. So overwhelming is the evidence of the resurrection that many hardcore skeptics have been convinced after thorough investigation of the facts.

Lew Wallace was one. An officer in the Mexican and Civil wars, and governor of New Mexico territory from 1878 to 1881, Wallace was one who openly discredited the claims of Christ. Yet, after thorough and honest research, he became a believer and the author of the famous Christian novel, *Ben Hur.*

Frank Morison, an English lawyer, was a skeptic who undertook to write a book proving once and for all that the resurrection was a myth. According to his own testimony, he studied the life of Christ "with a very definite feeling that . . . His history rested upon very insecure foundations." His attitude was that the historical Jesus never actually lived — that the Gospel records were nothing more than brilliant apologetics.

Deciding to write a report on the seven days before the crucifixion, Morison applied all his legal skill to "stripping it of its overgrowth of primitive beliefs and suppositions." But the more he studied, the more the "impossible" became apparent. Jesus did rise from the dead. He had been God in the flesh as He claimed.

When people say, 'I've lost my faith," they are really saying, "I'm not sure Jesus rose from the dead."

And with great power the apostles were giving witness to the resurrection of the Lord Jesus, and abundant grace was upon them all. Acts 4:33 NASB

Those who deny the Resurrection of Christ claim one of several things could have happened. Jesus may have only swooned; His disciples may have stolen His body to lend credence to their claim; the Roman authorities may have hidden the body; it was an apparition, not the real Jesus the disciples saw; it was mass hysteria — an hallucination.

If the Resurrection were a fraud, it was the most cleverly perpetrated deception in the annals of history. Over five hundred people professed to see Jesus after His death. Did they all conspire? If so, how was a secret of that magnitude kept among so great a number?

Did the disciples steal the body? If so, how? Roman sentries, charged with guarding the tomb at the cost of their own lives, would not have daydreamed or slept through an event that would have required several people to move back a monstrous stone and remove a corpse.

Did Rome dispose of the body? Ridiculous! They were as anxious as the Pharisees to keep His body entombed.

The most popular denial of the Resurrection claims that the disciples suffered hallucinations. They only thought He had returned from the dead because they had gone through certain pathological experiences in which they "saw" Jesus, although in reality He was not there. The disciples, however, were persuaded *against their wills* that Jesus had risen from the dead!

Mary came to the tomb that first Easter Sunday morning with spices to anoint His body. When the disciples first heard He had risen, they didn't believe it. Not until they touched Him and talked to Him were they convinced.

What effect did this have? It changed a band of cowardly disciples into men of courage and conviction. Peter, who had denied Jesus but a short time before, risked his life fifty days later by saying he had seen Him alive from the dead. All of the disciples except John paid for their testimonies with their lives.

We are not dealing with a theory. The Christian faith is not just another religious notion to be pulled out of the hat. We are dealing with a *living Man* who conquered death, ascended to heaven, and is coming back to judge the quick and the dead!

I beseech you therefore, brethren, by the mercies of God, that ye present your bodies a living sacrifice, holy, acceptable unto God, which is your reasonable service. Romans 12:1

Concepts regarding the purpose and importance of the human body have varied from century to century and generation to generation. The Victorians thought the body should be treated with distrust, distaste, and disgust. It was, to them, the seat of sin.

In recent decades, however, the pendulum has swung crazily to the opposite extreme. Today the body is regarded as a toy by the publishers of pornographic publications — a plaything to be exploited without regard to the human spirit within. Movies glorify every type of sexual gratification and perversion without portraying the inevitable payday for such flouting of the laws of God.

Question: how should the Christian regard his or her body? Should it be treated with respect, or resented? Should it be pampered or abused and neglected?

Whether we realize it or not, just about every plan we make for ourselves is closely associated with our inner health and our outward appearance. However we regard our bodies, they *are* the visible part of ourselves and a mighty precious and important possession.

If farmers keep their implements well oiled, greased, and sharpened; if wise doctors keep their instruments sharp and sterile; if athletes keep their bodies strong through discipline; surely Christians should present to God as their "reasonable service" bodies capable of serving Him for as long as possible. (See 1 Corinthians 9:24-27.)

Finally, our bodies are a trust given us by a wise and loving Father, and we are accountable to Him for our use of them. "For we shall all stand before the judgment seat of Christ . . . that everyone may receive the things done *in the body,* according to that he hath done, whether it be good or bad" 2 Corinthians 5:10.

Today Christ walks and works and speaks and carries out His eternal plan through human bodies, possessed and directed by His Holy Spirit. Because of this, should we not cherish and treat them with respect?

Your body is powerful — control it.
It is God's instrument — use it in His service.

Thou wilt show me the path of life; in thy presence is fulness of joy; at thy right hand there are pleasures forevermore.
Psalm 16:11

"Have a good time!" How often these parting words are spoken to friends, and the meaning is clear: *do what you want to do and find enjoyment in it.*

As a young man I found it hard to conceive that a Christian could really have a good time. I thought of God as a killjoy; some church people I knew were dull and grumpy. The minister's voice warned about God's punishment of the sinner, so to me, God and a good time were incompatible.

Later, of course, I discovered that this was a warped view; that it didn't reflect the picture of God given in the Bible. I came to know innumerable men, women, and young people who had discovered that living for God can be joyous — that it produces a zest and delight to which no rhetoric can do justice.

Jim Elliot was one of five brave young missionaries who gave their lives to reach the Auca Indians of Ecuador. Here is a page from his diary:

I walked out to the hill just now. It is exalting, delicious to stand embraced by the shadows of a friendly tree with the wind tugging at your coattail and the heavens hailing your heart; to gaze and glory and give oneself again to God. What more could a man ask?

Oh, the fullness, pleasure, sheer excitement of knowing God on earth. I care not if I ever raise my voice again for Him, if only I may love Him, please Him. Mayhap in mercy He shall give me a host of children that I may lead them through the vast star fields to explore His delicacies whose finger ends set them to burning. But if not, if only I may see Him, touch His garments, and smile into His eyes — ah, then, not stars, not children shall matter. Only Himself.

The Psalmist, too, praised God for His wonderful creation. Typical is this outburst of appreciation in Psalm 19: "The heavens are telling the glory of God; and the firmament proclaims His handiwork."

Jesus spoke of the happiness of a bride and groom, of the warm friendliness of a dinner invitation, of the rejoicing at birth of a baby, the lilies of the field.

We were made with the capacity to be happy. But happiness is unobtainable without Him.

And herein do I exercise myself, to have always a conscience void of offense toward God and toward men. Acts 24:16

The Bible teaches that each of us has a voice within us that registers the approach of moral danger. This "umpire" is God's built-in gift of conscience. Unless buried by insanity or slain by abuse, it is a restraining influence until the very moment of death.

Does this mean that however successfully we think conscience has been buried, it will assert itself again? Yes. It may be dulled, seared, or even buried, but it has a way of coming back. One day it may be silent, but the next, it accuses with murderous accuracy. Conscience, you see, is God's watchdog, His inner monitor. You may put it to sleep with some slick drug, but it will continue its vigilance. It is entirely capable of resurrection.

A great pulpiteer of the past century has suggested that the book to be opened on the day of judgment may be the book of conscience where misimproved opportunities, a lurid past, and unforgiven sin are forever recorded.

A number of years ago, in the state of Washington, a hitchhiker murdered the young man who had given him a ride. The body was found, but there was no trace of the slayer.

Several years passed. Then one evening, in a small Missouri town, a man came home from work to his wife and small son. Before he reached the door, a man stepped from the shadows and announced he was under arrest for murder. The youth dropped his lunch box and blurted out, "I've lived in hell these three years."

Confessing the crime, he added: "Every time I looked at that body I saw those dead eyes staring at me. They have stared at me day and night for these three years!"

By contrast, here is Paul's testimony to the Corinthian believers: "For our proud confidence is this, the testimony of our conscience that in holiness and godly sincerity . . . we have conducted ourselves in the world, and especially toward you" 2 Corinthians 1:12 NASB.

What is your conscience saying to you?

And this commandment we have from Him, that the one who loves God should love his brother also. 1 John 4:21 NASB

Nothing ever happens through us until something happens to us. How often I have seen the indwelling presence of Jesus Christ bring about a dramatic change in people. One man who experienced this inner change said, "I knew it was real because I lost all desire to go about trying to correct other people. I only wanted to accept, love, and help others."

This is the norm for people who allow Christ to have His way in their lives. When all hostility toward Him is gone, hostility toward others vanishes concurrently.

Personally, I have never met a Christian whom I could not love as a brother or sister, regardless of color, race, denomination, or political ties. When a person has peace with God through Jesus Christ, he cannot harbor animosity in his heart toward others for whom He died, and whom He loves equally. That would be like hating one's own mother or being at enmity with every member of his household.

This does not mean, of course, that we endorse everything others do. Jesus loved the world, but He didn't endorse it. However, we must strive to avoid letting the faults and failures of others alienate us from them, knowing that we wouldn't want ours to alienate them from us.

I'm thinking now of a Christian brother who, through no fault of his own, is sometimes repulsive—even obnoxious. He talks too much, and what he says is seldom worth listening to or remembering. But as I search my own heart concerning my brother, I conclude that I really love him. I don't say I would go out of my way to spend an evening with him; yet I see him as a man dear to the heart of God—saved just as I was saved—and undoubtedly doing the best he can with what he has been given.

This attitude should not be restricted only to fellow Christians but also to those whose appearance and lifestyle are repulsive to us. I imagine if we could have seen some of the characters Jesus stopped to heal, we would have seen nothing in them to love. But He did!

Why do you spend your money for that which is not bread, and your labor for that which does not satisfy? Isaiah 55:2 RSV

Dr. Clovis Chappel tells the story of the first Christmas party he ever attended as a Sunday school boy. The church was crowded; the Christmas tree was bright with candles and loaded with presents. Santa Claus walked among those present, distributing the gifts as the names were called.

Among the group was a mentally retarded boy who gazed upon the event with eager eyes. When everyone else had received presents, however, his name had not been called and he was the picture of dejection. Then suddenly Santa handed him the last and largest box under the tree.

Eagerly, and with a face mirroring great expectation, the boy opened it with nervous fingers, but soon his expression changed to one of pitiful despair. The box was empty. Someone had played a trick on him.

That's a horrifying story, but no more so than stories that happen to people every day. The world is actually full of empty boxes and all of us have taken our turns at playing the village idiot. We have reached for glittering things, spent our energies (maybe our characters) reaching for things we think we want, only to find we have empty boxes.

Remember how you told yourself you would be happy when you moved into that new trilevel or when you could have that Cadillac? Did they make you happy?

Those who search for happiness without God find every box empty. Do you want to know what is wrong with the world? We've built a superficial civilization on the lie that men can live by bread alone. The idea that we get a better world when we have high wages, good housing, and prosperous markets was exploded long ago. Stripped of the spiritual, these add up to empty boxes again.

The late Gilbert Chesterton wandered far from his faith. He said later he was like a man who had set off from the coast of England in search of a new island. After a hard, long voyage, he landed on the shores of what he thought was a new country, so he ran up his flag on the beach. But after looking around, the landscape looked familiar. It was the same sea coast from which he had departed.

This was his experience in the spiritual realm, also. He had scorned Christianity as a worn-out faith, only to discover that when he found faith, it was Christianity. Trying to escape from home, he came home!

Let us hold fast the profession of our faith without wavering; (for he is faithful that promised). Hebrews 10:23

The Bible says that faith in Jesus Christ is the doorway to heaven. If you ask whether this requires a special kind of faith, I'll have to answer yes . . . and no. Faith alone, or misplaced, means nothing. It is the *object* of faith that is all important.

It is important that faith come from the heart. Head faith is nothing more than mental assent, and in relation to Christ this could amount to as little as an approving nod that implies, "O.K., Jesus — I'm all for you!"

Christians, down through the centuries, are people who have "risked" Jesus, to use that expression reverently. One may read articles and books about conversion, but this is totally unavailing until one takes the step of faith — the "risk," if you will — of trusting Him personally.

Faith, you see, is the medium through which God makes it possible for human beings to become children of God (Ephesians 2:8, 9), and faith is something that is available to everybody. If salvation had been offered for good works, how many such works would be necessary? If for intellectual brilliance, the majority of earthlings would be eliminated. Good looks would certainly narrow the field. But everyone can come by faith.

Lord, give me faith — to trust, if not to know;
   With quiet mind in all things Thee to find;
And, childlike, go where Thou wouldst have me go.

Lord, give me faith to leave it all to Thee.
   The future is Thy gift; I would not lift
The vail Thy love has hung 'twixt it and me.

Why art thou cast down, O my soul? and why art thou disquieted in me? Psalm 42:5

In his interesting and informative book *A Touch of Greatness,* Harold Kohn explains the difference between climate and weather. Climate, he states, endures, while weather is momentary. Weather fluctuates; there are sudden changes in humidity, barometric pressure, cloudiness, temperature, and wind. But climate represents a long, enduring, prevailing characteristic — a pattern. It is the climate, not the weather, that determines which plants, insects, birds, and animals can grow in a region.

"The best climate," asserts Kohn, "can occasionally be assaulted with the worst weather!"

Now, the climate of the Christian life is good — in fact, wonderful. Most Christians I know feel every day that it's great to be a Christian. This is the "climate" in which they live. But sometimes the "weather" gets pretty rough, and because Christians are still human, there may be second thoughts.

I've seen some radiant believers fall into some mighty dark moods. Their "weather" upsets their usually dependable "climate."

I've learned through experience that the child of God should never allow bad "weather" to upset the tempo of his or her life. Furthermore, important decisions should never be made during a "storm." When it passes, and it will, one may find that a tragedy has been evaded by postponing a life-changing decision until it could be evaluated more objectively.

Have you ever noticed how hard it is to visualize the sun during a torrential rain? But it will shine again, and today's depression will give way to joy on the morrow. Go to God for help; immerse yourself in His Word. Seek the strength that is to be found in His presence.

Peter, the volatile disciple, gives some practical advice in his first epistle: "Casting all your care upon him [Christ] for he careth for you" (5:7). If you do that — not just occasionally but on a regular basis — very little bad weather will be able to creep into the climate of your life.

. . . What has happened to me has really served to advance the gospel. Philippians 1:12 RSV

Despite the dangers involved, millions of "sun-worshipers" expose themselves to the relentless solar rays of the sun, frying like hot dogs on a barbecue spit. And all for the questionable advantage of obtaining a glorious tan.

Why do some people tan and others burn? Because human skin contains a pigment called melanin. If the epidermis produces enough of this substance, a tan will result. If too little, the result will be a burn. In other words, what happens to you in the sun depends on you — not the sun.

Let's apply that principle to life. Some people just cave in under adversity. They become resentful, blame God and society, and give up. Others refuse to let hardship embitter them. They win a continual inner victory. Some tan and some burn!

We have little control over our troubles, but we have a lot of control over our response to them. Consider this incident in the lives of Paul and Silas. While preaching the gospel in Philippi, they were apprehended by the authorities and thrown into prison. They were beaten and placed in stocks, but they prayed and sang!

God permitted two of His most faithful, effective servants to be thrown into prison, not to punish them, but so the world could see the difference between tanning and burning. Would you have burned or tanned under that sun?

THE SEARCH

I sought Him in a great cathedral, dim
With age, where oft-repeated prayers arise,
But caught no glimpse of Him.

I sought Him then atop a lonely hill,
Like Moses once, but tho' I scanned the skies,
My search was fruitless still.

There was a little home where grief and care
Had bred but courage, love, and valiant will.
I sought — and found Him there.

— Anne Marriott

Husbands, love your wives even as Christ also loved the church, and gave himself for it. Ephesians 5:25

Despite America's sad deterioration, we are still known the world over as "the land of the free." Why are we still the envy of other countries? Because we are a product of Christian principles and foreign missions.

Let me tell you something you may not know. During the colonial days, societies in Europe raised money and supported missionaries here for years, until those churches became strong enough to support themselves. One organization called *The Society for Propagating the Gospel in Foreign Parts* sent 310 missionaries to the colonies, and organized more than 200 mission centers, out of which many churches eventually grew. Not many history courses mention that, but it is definitely a part of our national heritage.

So America is a child of foreign mission. Others were motivated to share their faith with us, and this contributed to our greatness as a nation. Every "Women's Lib" enthusiast should take a long, hard look at those nations where women are little more than beasts of burden, where evangelical Christianity has not penetrated. They will find that the Bible, instead of belittling womanhood, elevates it!

Women were influential in Jesus' background. Women were the first converts in Europe, including the prosperous businesswoman, Lydia, in Philippi. Those who suggest that the Bible subjugates women are either unfamiliar with Scripture or irrationally hostile toward it. What greater dignity could be bestowed upon women than to have the Church referred to as the bride of Christ? Furthermore, the Bible states that a married man no longer owns his own body, but that it belongs to his wife. I would say that no teaching could go further in elevating women.

At the turn of the century, master pulpiteer T. DeWitt Talmage said:

In lands where there is no Bible [woman] is hitched like a beast of burden to the plow; she carries the hod; she submits to indescribable indignities.

Why does a woman, when she is trouble, go to the Bible? Why not to some infidel books?

The Bible is not only *for* the liberation of women: it authored it!

I will be merciful toward their iniquities, and I will remember their sins no more. Hebrews 8:12 RSV

I doubt that the punishment known as "drumming out" is used any longer in the military. It dates back to a 17th-century English Army practice and it was used during the Civil War by both the North and South to discourage shirkers and deserters.

A young United States marine was court-martialed for larceny and found guilty. A sergeant major read the bad conduct discharge aloud, then snapped the order: "Escort this man from the confines of the United States Navy reservation!"

The bareheaded, disgraced marine was then led slowly past rows of marines standing at attention while the drummer beat the Rogue's March. As he passed each platoon, the servicemen turned from him in an about-face.

I'm glad God doesn't turn us away from His mercy when we sin. Instead, His love and compassion for the sinner are symbolized by the Father's open arms and the welcoming feast. The prodigal was not "drummed out" when he repented.

Let me ask you a simple, but very important, question. Are you on speaking terms with God? If not, it doesn't make sense to go on this way, does it? Listen to His invitation — and His promise: "Let the wicked forsake his way, and the unrighteous man his thoughts: and let him return unto the Lord, and he will have *mercy* upon him; and to our God, for he will abundantly *pardon*" Isaiah 55:7.

No "drumming out" — just mercy and pardon!

Anyone who hates his brother is a murderer, and you know that no murderer has eternal life in him. 1 John 3:15 RSV

Most of us know what it means to harbor ill will—to smolder inside with an intense animosity toward something or someone. As a minister of the Gospel, I have sometimes offended people, and people have offended me. But it would take a pretty vitriolic and sustained attack to make me forget a valuable lesson I have learned.

Once, a very long time ago, I became so disturbed over a certain man's treatment of me that I could think of little else all day long. It wasn't until much later that I learned this person was having the time of his life with me. He was letting me do the worrying and fuming for both of us. I had actually become a pawn in the hands of a man who was taking his spite out on God—through me!

You see, the moment we allow someone to rile us, that person becomes our master and we become his or her slave. "If someone strikes you on the cheek," said Jesus in Luke 6:29, "turn to him the other also." Again, He told His followers in Luke 6:37, "Forgive . . . and you shall be forgiven." If there is one thing that should characterize the Christian, it is forgiveness.

Paul, writing to the believers at Corinth, reminded them that love is not easily angered; *it keeps no record of wrongs.* That means no brooding, no licking of wounds, no gossiping about real or imagined slights or ill treatment.

Any inability or unwillingness on our part to cross off the wrongs we have suffered is a clear indication of our own spiritual poverty.

Study to show yourself approved unto God, a workman that needs not to be ashamed, rightly dividing the Word of truth.
2 Timothy 2:15

When someone says the Bible is not true, that the current acquisition of knowledge has exploded and outmoded it, I want to know who's doing the talking. I want him or her to show me credentials. I want to know how much that person really knows about the Book, how honest has been the research applied to the discovery of Very Truth.

Has that individual ever, in honesty and humility, asked God to reveal Himself through Jesus Christ? Only after I have at least this much information will I be able to form a dispassionate judgment as to his or her credentials.

The Bible was given us to read, and also to study. It would be interesting to know the percentage of critics who have actually studied the Bible, looking into the original texts and straightening out some of the archaic English expressions which were more meaningful in the 17th century than they are to modern readers. One deeply suspects the skeptic of bias bordering on a closed mind!

A vast world lies beyond us which science cannot see, understand, or explain, but which the Bible reveals. Let us not think we can destroy this spiritual world by disavowing it.

I believe the Bible because it has been my constant companion for over half a century, during which time it has never let me down. It has never strained or disappointed my intellect; it has never promised anything it could not deliver; it has never failed to answer a question or solve a problem. These are my reasons for believing it, revering it, protecting it, and preaching it. For these reasons I shall die with my faith resting in it.

Father, forgive them; for they know not what they do. Luke 23:34

A man once said to me, "I would very much like to know that my sins are forgiven, but I can't take your word for it; in fact, I can't even take the word of the Bible. It all sounds too easy."

That man didn't know much about the nature of forgiveness.

Suppose a son does everything possible to hurt and shame his father. He forges checks; he spends most of his time in jail; he runs away from home; he cracks up the car in a drunken driving spree. But one day he appears at the door of his father's home and says, "Dad, I've made a mess of my life. I want to straighten up and make amends. Will you take me back . . . forgive me?"

What real father would turn down a plea like that? His door and his arms would be wide open to take back his penitent son.

But who would suggest that such an act of forgiveness was "easy"? Would the son say to his friends, "My dad's an easy mark"? Not if his repentance were sincere. His father's forgiveness would be the most moving experience of his life.

Keep in mind, however, that forgiveness is predicated on an admission of wrongdoing. It is never "easy." One must become rather like a beggar to be forgiven. And only one who has been *hurt* can forgive. When Jesus said on the cross, "Father, forgive them, for they know not what they do," He was the offended One. He was asking the Father to forgive those who were killing Him. There was nothing cheap or easy about that.

If we really want forgiveness, how can we be sure this has taken place? Not only because His Word says so, but because the knowledge of it builds up in our hearts and minds like a strange hunch, and we find ourselves thanking Him for the accomplished fact of 1 John 1:9: "If we confess our sins, he is faithful and just to forgive us our sins and to cleanse us from all unrighteousness."

. . . Absent from the body, . . . present with the Lord.
2 Corinthians 5:8

A florist's truck bears this sign: *Crosses and Wreaths Made to Order.* Actually, we have more to say about the size and shape of our burdens than we think. When sorrow comes, as it does and will, we have the choice of shouldering it all by ourselves, or admitting it is too big for us and taking it to the Lord.

I have personally done it both ways. I recommend the latter.

Please understand that I am not minimizing the grief of bereavement. Jesus Himself wept over the death of His friend Lazarus, even while knowing He would soon restore him to life. Teardrops are not sin, unless they represent unassuagable grief. Perpetual anguish is the same as telling God He has made a mistake, that you question His sovereignty.

Carl Sandburg, in his work on the life of Abraham Lincoln, *The Prairie Years,* said that the early settlers buried their loved ones with their own hands and shovels because there were no neighbors near when fever struck them down. All that kept the survivors going was their Christian faith. When preachers came to town, they would gather, and in Sandburg's words, "wash their souls in revival."

Sorrow? Yes, of course, but tempering those sorrows are the unshakable promises of God and the comfort of One who came to this earth and suffered heartaches and indignities and burdens you and I will never be called upon to bear. It is to Him we must turn for comfort in the anguished hours.

When you have a headache, the science of chemistry can help you. When you have a toothache, the science of dentistry can help you. But when you have a heartache, only the Great Physician can help you.

Have you taken your need for comfort to Him?

The Word was made flesh, and dwelt among us. John 1:14

Empathy differs from sympathy in that it implies actually experiencing the feelings of another. To sympathize with another is to have compassion; to empathize is to place oneself vicariously in the particular place or circumstances of the other person.

Jesus is able to empathize with us because He put Himself in a state similar to ours. "He was in all points tempted like as we are, yet without sin," we read in Hebrews 4:15.

Perhaps the greatest weakness in the gospel ministry today reflects our failure to learn the "language" of people's hearts. Because our own hands are clean, we can't understand those whose hands are dirty. We listen only to those whose sermons reflect our own convictions; therefore, when someone comes from a totally different background, we are helpless. Since we don't know the way they think, we can't understand what they are saying.

Jesus spoke in parables so men could see and feel what He was talking about. Otherwise, would the crowds have followed Him, hanging on His every word? His divine empathy drew them to Himself. He loved them, and they understood it.

Listen, God doesn't speak to man from an armchair. He speaks from a cross. He empathizes with us because He sat where we sit!

The Indian has a prayer that goes something like this: "Great Spirit, help me never to judge another until I have walked two weeks in his moccasins." That is a good prayer, no matter to whom it is addressed!

As newborn babes, desire the sincere milk of the word, that ye may grow thereby. 1 Peter 2:2

No one grows because he determines to do so, nor can an individual stop growing simply by setting his mind to it. We are all a part of an astounding process taking place all over the world in the simplest to the most complex forms of life. Something called growth is happening invisibly and mysteriously, whether within a lily or a child, that remains inexplicable.

The maturing of the mind is similar to that of the body, with the greatest difference lying in one's own volition to stimulate mental growth. Naturally, we don't awaken one morning and say, "Mind, today you become brilliant!" Mental development in the human race is a long, slow, and often tortuous process, reaching its zenith when we admit that life's mysteries far exceed its revelations.

Our God-given mental faculties were meant to be developed by us to their fullest potential, and it is within our jurisdiction to do so. However, it is equally possible for us to prostitute, warp, and retard our minds until we resemble the pagans described in Romans 1 who "became futile in their thinking and their senseless minds were darkened" (vs. 21 RSV).

But there is another area of growth, and this also comes from God: spiritual growth. Here, too, development may be volitionally retarded if we so choose. In his second letter, Peter prods his readers to "grow in grace, and in the knowledge of our Lord and Savior Jesus Christ" (3:18).

How do we grow spiritually? Certainly not by saying, "I will grow!" Spiritual growth takes place as a byproduct of taking spiritual nourishment (God's Word) and spiritual exercise (prayer). Food and exercise. This is not an oversimplification. If we devote ourselves to these essentials, we will find ourselves *growing in grace* without even being aware of it.

I tell you, this sinner, not the Pharisee, returned home forgiven.
Luke 18:14 TLB

One of the most interesting and informative parables our Lord ever told concerns two men, one of whom is a religious leader, and the other a crook.

The Pharisee is representative of those who are wholly satisfied with themselves. To be honest, generous, and religious is not something for which a person should be censured. We want to credit the Pharisee with everything that is right about him, but he had one overriding fault: he refused to see himself through God's eyes. He was self-righteous.

I have met such people — and you have, too. The gospel of God's grace doesn't phase them. because, in their opinion, there is no need for His atonement. Pharisees feel less need for the services of the church than a healthy man feels for medicine.

There is a problem, however. The Bible clearly says, "Christ Jesus came into the world to save *sinners.*" A Christian is one who has realized that he or she was too evil to receive salvation on the basis of personal merit and who has sought out Jesus Christ as a sick man seeks out a doctor. Actually, both the Pharisee and the publican were victims of the same disease of sin. The difference was that while the Pharisee prayed, "I thank thee that I am not as other men are . . . or even as this publican," the publican smote on his breast, saying, "God be merciful to me, *a sinner!*" Jesus said, "I tell you, this man went down to his house *justified.*"

A popular bumper sticker says it well: "Christians aren't perfect — just *forgiven.*

From everlasting to everlasting, thou art God. Psalm 90:2

The human mind looks backward until the past vanishes, then forward until thought and imagination collapse from exhaustion, and God is there at both points. Man, a creature of time, grapples helplessly with any concept of eternity, past or future. Even when he guesses the age of the earth, he must express it in terms of years, for they represent the only concepts his mind can comprehend.

But these measurements do not apply to God, for He is not subject to time or space. Isaiah describes Him as "the high and lofty One that inhabiteth eternity" (57:15).

We cannot conceive of anything that cannot be measured, for measurement is the only way created things have of accounting for themselves. Measurement is man's method of describing abilities, limitations, or imperfections. But there is no kind of measurement we can apply to God, for He is limitless and perfect. With our limited concepts we embrace men, mountains, stars, atoms, gravity, energy, numbers, and speed; but God fits into none of these categories. It cannot be said that something is "easy" or "hard" for Him.

Pollsters tell us that the vast majority of earthlings believe in God. Many understand their "God" because they have created him in their minds. But if your God never astonishes you, never transcends you, then He is not the God of the Bible who sent His Son to earth to ransom Adam's sinful race.

. . . and whatever my eyes desired I did not keep from them; I kept my heart from no pleasure . . . and behold, all was vanity and a striving after the wind. . . . Ecclesiastes 2:10, 11 RSV

Poor wise, stupid Solomon! He forgot that he was a spiritual, as well as a physical being. His was a theory, now seeing its revival, that it is harmful to frustrate a natural instinct or suppress a normal desire.

He had not learned that happiness lies in the harmonizing of all desires.

Let me tell you why any dream of a good world without God and without restrictions is delusive. It just won't work! Let the prodigal son tell about it, or the millions of others who have indulged in that folly. There is a Law — a silent imperative in nature — that stands in the road with upraised hand and cries, "Stop! This is not the way to life!" Something akin to gravity takes over and the dream explodes in your face.

This is because we are mortal. Thrills play out, sensations are short-lived, pleasures pall. Solomon made happiness a business and he worked hard at it. He surrounded himself with every pleasure the senses could provide, but one day he added it up and got zero! Like many today, he was trying to satisfy his desire for ease and comfort at the expense of another part of him that demanded he do something significant, something creative, something eternal.

Man is always in torment when he is out of fellowship with his Maker.

Are you lonely, discontented, restless, fed up? Then thank God! Someone is whispering in your soul, "Remember you are immortal, and restless will be your heart until you rest in Me."

Ask and ye shall receive, that your joy may be full. John 16:24

Happiness has been described as a word around whose flavor and fragrance human hopes have hovered since the beginning of time. It is so intensely desirable that it would be very strange if we were given no clue as to its meaning and availability.

Theologians are fond of pointing out that the word "happy" appears only a few times in the Bible, and then it does not apply to spirituality. Nevertheless, the word "blessed" occurs at least two hundred times, and in most cases it is the equivalent of our English word "happy."

The nine "blesseds" Jesus used in His Beatitudes seem to provide evidence that happiness is the common heritage of those who love and obey Him. Note, however, that this happiness is not dependent on outward circumstances. "Blessed are the merciful . . . the meek . . . the hungry . . . the persecuted . . . those who mourn" — an odd assemblage to represent the ultimate in joy. However, they portray a supernatural quality that is not dependent upon outward pressures.

While many today are claiming that happiness is man's inalienable right and should be pursued at all costs, the Bible teaches that happiness is a bonus we receive while we are pursuing something else. That is why true happiness can be likened to the ocean depth. While thirty-foot waves rock the ships on the surface, only a few yards below there is utter tranquility.

Happiness cannot be purchased at the supermarket or ordered by mail. It is a gift, offered by Jesus Christ to those who follow Him. On the night of His betrayal, He revealed what lay ahead for Him, and for them. At the same time He bequeathed them something that could never be taken from them. Listen: "Ye now therefore have sorrow: but I will see you again, and your heart shall rejoice, and your joy no man taketh from you" John 16:22.

Jesus wasn't a killjoy, my friend. He is the source of joy, and He has provided it for all who will follow him. But it's up to you to appropriate it for yourself.

Your heart shall rejoice, and your joy no man taketh from you.
John 16:22

Jesus, by every standard normally applied to life, should have been an
unhappy person. "Foxes have holes," He said, "and the birds of the air
have nests; but the Son of man hath not where to lay his head"
Matthew 8:20. That level of poverty is not calculated to make a person
uncontrollably ecstatic; nor was the treatment He received at the
hands of His enemies. Yet the writer of Hebrews speaks of "the joy
that was set before him" (12:2).

To His disciples, Jesus said, "These things have I spoken unto you
that my joy might remain in you, and that your joy might be full" John
15:11. He was referring, of course, to 1) His being taken from them in
death and 2) to their joy at seeing Him come forth from the grave.

If His resurrection was to be a source of inward joy to them, why not
to us?

Americans are, corporately, an unhappy people. Ours is a nation
wallowing in affluence, spending billions on things to do, places to
go, and stuff to swallow. With the highest living standard in the world,
most people are miserable. Why? Because the most bored,
maladjusted people are those who seek happiness on the physical
level, bulldozing their way through God's moral laws regardless of
what effect it has on society.

But man's physical drives are but a fragment of his total self. True
fulfillment in life consists not of asking, "What do I want?" but "What
is wanted of me?"

Jesus said, "Happy are the pure in heart, for they shall see God"
Matthew 5:8.

I sink in deep mire, where there is no standing: I am come into deep waters, where the floods overflow me. Psalm 69:2

A small girl dropped and broke her favorite doll. Tearfully, she picked it up and was heard t. lament, "I'm so sorry for me!"

We all have much in common with that little lady. At times we have a tendency to submerge ourselves in self-pity. I have known very few in my kind of ministry who did not, periodically, feel overworked, abused, and worthy of more credit than they have received. The one I know best? Myself.

If you read the Psalms you will discover that David spent a good deal of time feeling sorry for himself. He seemed to fluctuate between spiritual highs and lows — times of victory and times of deepest gloom. Most of us can empathize with him on both levels.

Satan's ploy from earliest times is to get believers to magnify their problems and minimize their spiritual resources. As a result, self-pity gives us a distorted concept of the world around us and our purpose in it.

I once read of an office worker who pretended to have more assignments and a heavier load of responsibility than anyone else in his place of business. He stayed night after night long after the others had gone home. But it was a hoax to gain sympathy. His employers expected no more of him than they did of the others.

Do you feel like a martyr? Honestly, now, wouldn't it be a lot better if you just thanked God for putting you here at this particular point in time, knowing that you have the ability to adapt and be happy if you focus on good mental and spiritual attitudes?

Wouldn't it be a lot better to get together with others and thank God for life, however hard it may seem?

Your life can be a blight or a blessing; it all depends on you. God has promised that when you walk through the waters they will not overflow you (Isaiah 43:2). Believe it, and stop pitying yourself!

Let us not be desirous of vainglory, provoking one another, envying one another. Galatians 5:26

One dictionary defines jealousy as "the emotion aroused by the presentation of enjoyment on the part of another under conditions considered desirable for oneself." This explanation reveals the three factors always present in jealousy: 1) something we want; 2) a competitor; 3) a stirred-up emotional state.

Judgment is withered by jealousy; it makes people do things they would not otherwise think of doing. It can drive normally stable people to inflict bodily injury on another, or even commit murder. Many a home is a little vestibule of hell because of jealousy.

Unfortunately, there is no quick or easy cure for this deadly malady. We cannot be delivered from pettiness by memorizing a set of rules or resolving to be different. Even reading a message on the subject, as you are doing now, is ineffective unless God is allowed to plant His love in our hearts and transform us by His Spirit. Otherwise, we will continue to be manipulated by "the jaundiced eye."

Let me suggest three ways by which you can *begin* the process of taming the beast of jealousy:

Reappraise your standard of success. Jealousy is the confession of the failure of your value system. Remember, the goal of life is not happiness, but holiness; not acquisition, but service. A server is never a failure, or a jealous person.

Don't compare yourself with others. Jesus taught that talents are distributed at the discretion of the Creator. Some people are given five, some two, some only one. Not all were born to be executives. What another is, or has, should not concern us. We are to develop whatever God has seen fit to entrust to us.

Be generous. We must learn the grace of giving to others and jealousy cannot exist in such an atmosphere.

Remember, you cannot rout jealousy by yourself. Only the Holy Spirit can give you the power to rejoice in the good that comes to another, and His power is released on your behalf through prayer and obedience to the Word of God.

Let the redeemed of the Lord say so. Psalm 107:2

I gather from our verse that there is one subject at least that pleases God and concerning which we cannot talk too much. It's the topic of redemption.

The failure of so many Christians to speak out on this magnificent truth has been referred to as "sinful reticence." No such timidity is manifested when it comes to a discussion of politics, neighborhood gossip, tensions in the Middle East, or the drug traffic. People talk copiously on such topics, but when it comes to sharing their experience of conversion and the hope of heaven, there is often a chilling silence.

Have you been blessed by a book, a sermon, a testimony, an act of friendship . . . a life? Then say so. Speak up!

There are ways other than words to express oneself — to "say so." Some witness by writing to shut-ins, visiting the needy, sharing their substance with those less fortunate. A vast army of the redeemed keeps the Word of the Lord going out from their churches and over the airwaves. Through their generous giving (often sacrificially) missionaries are able to take the message of God's love to those who have never heard of Christ.

A Christian woman once said to her pastor, "My days of usefulness are over. I don't know why God lets me continue to live. I'm no help to Him or anyone else."

He replied, "Let me correct you. You inspire me every Sunday by your faithful attendance. You are more alert than all the rest; you look right up at me and listen intently and that's an inspiration to do my best. Occasionally a tear courses down your cheek, and this lets me know my message has reached your heart. You are important to me." She had been "speaking up."

Yes, Christians "say so" in many ways, and through their witness whole neighborhoods are being changed. Society doesn't appreciate such people. The world has no praise for them. But someday God will commend those whose priorities in this life have been to glorify Him who loved them and gave Himself for them.

Meanwhile, let's keep "speaking up."

. . . the aged men [should] be grave, temperate, sound in faith, in charity, in patience. The aged women likewise, [should] be in behaviour as becometh holiness . . . teachers of good things.
Titus 2:2, 3

Adjusting to old age is never easy. Yet we must all bravely and realistically face the inevitable and the way we accomplish this depends upon our outlook as individuals.

I have personally grappled with the problem of growing older, and perhaps some of my findings will be helpful to you. Let's give it a try, anyway.

1. First, let's be certain we are majoring in spirituality in our sunset years. The spiritually mature person never wears his or her feelings on the coatsleeve or asks to be waited on. Rather there is a desire to help others with humility, honesty, kindness, and understanding. Such a one doesn't give in to depression or nurture real or imagined "hurts."

2. Don't give up living! Resist a steady diet of "precious memories." Nothing is gained by fingering our memories every day like a rosary. It's all right to spend fifteen minutes on them, but not fifteen years!

3. Serve. At any age we must concentrate on helping others. Write letters, visit, grow vegetables or flowers and share them with someone.

4. Don't let life become empty. Stay mentally and spiritually alert. Don't begin every sentence with, "When I was young . . ." Live on! Don't forfeit the zest of meeting new experiences. Make new friends; read; keep abreast of your world.

5. Prepare for the long journey you will soon be taking. Don't come to the end of life without the glorious, stabilizing hope that is found only in Jesus Christ.

I have observed that the Spirit of God is able to transform age as easily and dramatically as youth. God does not abandon the aged unless at their own bidding. If you feel forsaken, beset by fears and regrets, Christ cares. He will come into your life if you ask Him and will flood your closing days with His presence.

Thou sayest, I am rich and increased with goods, and have need of nothing; and knowest not that thou art wretched, and miserable, and poor, and blind, and naked. Revelation 3:17

Is there really any sense to life? Who are we? What are we doing here?

Most people who are asking these questions are demanding pat, easy answers. They don't object to enough religion to make them comfortable—to ease their twinges of conscience—but they want God in a giant, economy size box at a bargain price!

What many fail to realize is that the symbol of the Christian faith is a cross, and a cross is painful. God will never be found among all the fleshly indulgences to which most people persistently cling. I urge those who really want to experience Him to examine the price tag!

A successful young executive with a beautiful home, three cars, a speed boat, and a fine family, confided to a counselor: "It's all a fake. My business is based on buttering people up, feeding their egos. My home, boat, cars, are all props for making more money. Even my marriage is a fake. My wife and I play our roles for the sake of the children, but down deep there is nothing honest, nothing real."

Pascal, the 17th-century mathematician, philosopher, and author, declared: "There is a God-shaped vacuum in the heart of every person which only God can fill through His Son, Jesus Christ."

I can empathize with that statement. I, too, was an empty, searching youngster and not until someone introduced me to Jesus Christ did I find any sense or meaning to life. Then, and only then, I discovered that the God who brought creation out of chaos can bring someone flattened by failure to a faith that glues him to reality.

. . . the law requires that nearly everything be cleansed with blood, and without the shedding of blood there is no forgiveness. Hebrews 9:22 NIV

What this passage clearly means is that there is no forgiveness (or atonement) for sins without blood being shed on behalf of the guilty party. No matter how repugnant this concept may be to the self-righteous, self-sufficient pseudo-intellectual mind, the fact remains that this is God's edict, and it stands.

This principle of propitiation began in Eden the moment Adam and Eve partook of the forbidden fruit, became aware of their nakedness, and tried to clothe themselves with aprons of fig leaves. When God made coats for them from the skins of animals, obviously those animals were slain in order for the covering to be provided.

To put it bluntly, God sees one of two things when He looks at us — a makeshift fig-leaf apron, or His coat of skins.

The Wycliffe Bible Encyclopedia sums up the act of atonement in this way:

It was an act of redemption in which the price paid by another, and finally by God himself, was the precious blood of Christ. It was an act of conquest in which the powers of evil, sin, death, the devil and hell, were overthrown.

It was an act of sacrificial propitiation in which the pleasing, self-offering of the Innocent One was accepted representatively for the guilty. It was an act of penal judgment in which the divine wrath was suffered by the Just for the unjust; therefore, in one act, God was just and yet also the justifier of those who trust in Jesus Christ.

Charles Wesley (1707-1778) is known not only for his work as an evangelist but for his hymns, among them the well-loved Oh, For a Thousand Tongues. The last verse is a classic description of the Atonement:

He breaks the power of cancelled sin,
    He sets the prisoner free;
His blood can make the foulest clean;
    His blood availed for me.

They that are whole need not a physician; but they that are sick.
Matthew 9:12

The whole idea of separation as interpreted down through the years I was developing as a Christian, was to give the non-Christian a wide berth. The attitude of the believer was summed up in "taste not, see not, hear not; and if believers don't come *our* way, let them go to the hell they deserve!"

Well, maybe it's time we pay attention to Jesus' methods. He went to where the people were who needed Him most. "Why do you eat and drink with publicans and sinners?" He was asked. His answer: "They that are whole need not a physician, but they that are sick." Jesus, the Great Physician, sought out the ailing.

"But," someone will argue, "the Bible teaches separation. It says, 'If any man love the world, the love of the Father is not in him.' " Indeed it does (1 John 2:15) but we're talking about loving the *worldly*, and that's something else.

However, the "worldly" often avoid Christians, so how are we to demonstrate love? The obvious solution is for us to go to them — not to partake of their lifestyle, but to let them know we love them despite our differences.

Are Christians to love the world system and its values? Absolutely not.

Are we to love those outside of Christ? Unequivocally yes.

Are we to wait for them to come to us? No.

Are we to go to them? Yes.

Those who have dared to do so have known the exquisite joy of serving as ambassadors for Christ in an alien environment.

Moreover whom he did predestinate, them he also called: and whom he called, them he also justified: and whom he justified, them he also glorified. Romans 8:30

I believe that the Christian life consists of a plan, a divine plan. I stand firm in the belief that a perfect, just, detailed, and eternal purpose is in effect for those who belong to God through Jesus Christ.

Moreover, I believe that God knew, in the ages past, that a baby boy would be born to Benjamin and Bernice Jess in Chicago, Illinois, that he would, at age nineteen, receive Christ as his personal Savior, and that in the ensuing years he would become a pastor, an evangelist, and a radio minister.

But I also believe that God knew you would be born, would live the life you have lived, and that on this very day you would be reading these words. There is no way, you see, to put a fence around God or limit His knowledge, past or present. Admit God, and impossibility throws up its hands.

Here's the bad news: I believe it is possible for Satan to thwart God's plans when he finds a willing subject. Here's the good news: "Greater is He who is in you than he who is in the world." God is stronger than Satan!

Literature majors are taught that, ideally, an author has five points to a story, and they occur in this order: 1) Introduction; 2) rising action; 3) climax; 4) declining action; 5) conclusion. Not so for the children of God. To the believer, death is merely a comma, and when it finally appears on the record, the Father moves His child to another and perfect part of His domain to live with Him forever.

That's the planned life He provides for those who receive Him into their lives by faith — predestinated, called, justified, and glorified! What could be more exciting?

> The Lord is nigh unto them that are of a broken heart; and saveth such as be of a contrite spirit. Psalm 34:18

Today, in the maze of religious chaos and an infiltration of strange doctrines, many are asking, "How can I find God, if He can be found?"

First, let me assure you that God can be discovered, but there are conditions. One doesn't just rub a magic lamp and expect to have Him materialize. God has laid down certain conditions for "finding" Him and the first is a desire for purity and forgiveness. One doesn't strut up to God, thumbs in armpits, and say, "All right, let's see You perform!"

God, you see, reveals Himself to those who seek Him whole-heartedly, with an attitude that is receptive, contrite, humble, and hungry. While there is nothing in the Bible that implies one must do penance, repentance is essential.

How do we find God? Certainly not by doing something for Him. That comes after we have found Him. If we were able to see ourselves as He sees us, sinful and unworthy, we wouldn't have the temerity to try to gain His favor through human effort.

Finally, don't make the fatal mistake of by-passing Jesus Christ in your search for God. He is our Advocate with the Father, and only through His death, His blood, can we receive forgiveness of sins.

HIS HANDS

The hands of Christ
  Seem very frail,
For they were broken
  By a nail.

But only they
  Reach heaven at last
Whom those frail, broken
  Hands hold fast.

— John Richard Moreland

He chose us in him before the foundation of the world.
Ephesians 1:4

What was I made for? The question is neither stupid or irrelevant. It should be asked, and answered. We have a right to know why we are here, apart from the biological reason, and where we fit in the scheme of things.

This being the case, God is the One to ask. He alone understands what has been happening through the centuries in our ancestral lineage; He knows the genetic code that makes us what we are, and He alone is capable of taking into account everything that pertains to our dispositions, aptitudes, and destinies.

If you will make it a point to discover the purpose for which God permitted your entry into the world, you will avoid serious mistakes. Obviously we were not all created to be ministers, missionaries, or full-time Christian workers. There are men and women in medicine today who were as divinely called to that work as the person who has been called to the pulpit. In every legitimate profession there are those who were divinely appointed to that work. Wherever you serve, you can honor and glorify His name.

"But what can I do?" you ask. Well, you can do anything and everything you *should* do. You may come to the end of life, having fallen short of your highest ambition, but if you seek divine guidance and obey His leading, you can stand unashamed when you meet your Lord.

So do what you can for Him, and do it with all your might. Comfort that bereaved neighbor; tell her about the Christian's hope. Go to that man who is worrying himself sick about finances; tell him about the everlasting riches of those who love God. If you can sing, sing for that friend who won't be getting well. Maybe you can help him or her into heaven.

Dedicate your brain, your tongue, your eyes, your heart — your entire body, mind, and soul to God. You will discover that you were made for something *important*. Common sense says so. History says so. Experience says so. Faith says so. The Bible says so!

Blessed is the man that trusteth in the Lord, and whose hope the Lord is. Jeremiah 17:7

Just what is hope? The dictionary defines it as "desire accompanied by expectation of fulfillment." For hope to be stronger than mere desire it must be based not only on possibility, but reality.

Actually, few things in this life provide hope based on total assurance. Over the past few hundred years, "permanent" peace pacts have lasted an average of two years!

What, then, comprises the "sure" hope of the Christian? Paul defines it as "Christ in you, the hope of glory" Colossians 1:27. Not just an acceptance of Christ as an actual historical character; not belief in Him as a great and good man. "Christ in you" — a resurrected Christ, alive now and indwelling those who trust in Him. Peter calls it a living hope based on the resurrection of Christ from the dead (1 Peter 1:3).

Dr. Harold G. Wolff once conducted a survey for the Cornell University Medical School on the effects of hope on the body. His conclusions: "When a man has hope, he is capable of incredible burdens and the taking of cruel punishment."

Remember, the hope of the Christian is more than a spark of anticipation, a mere wish. It is expectation based on the reality of solid hope.

And every man that hath this hope in him purifieth himself, even as he is pure. 1 John 3:3

It is enough; now, O Lord, take away my life. 1 Kings 19:4

If those words sound as if they were spoken by a very disappointed man, it's because they were. Elijah was so disappointed and frightened he begged to die. But God had planned that Elijah wouldn't die at all, but would be taken to heaven in a blazing chariot with wheels of flame and horses of fire! When the day came for that wonderful event, Elijah must have been grateful that his childish, cowardly prayer was not answered.

We regret this dark chapter in the life of a great and godly man. We wish he had stood up to the imperious queen who had threatened to kill him. The Bible, however, is a book written about human beings as they were, not as they should have been. Elijah whimpered, "It is enough; now, O Lord, let me die." But God didn't say, "It is enough." Elijah may have been through with life, but God wasn't through with Elijah. The reason: God knew the future and Elijah didn't!

Perhaps you are asking right now, "Does God care? If so, why did He allow this to happen to me?"

Maybe you have suffered thwarted ambition, blighted dreams. Perhaps you have tried to reach the top rung of your professional ladder, only to see another pass and surpass you, leaving you a relatively mediocre and disappointed person. Maybe your health is broken and nothing known to medical science holds out any hope for you, so you are asking, "Does God care?"

Let me tell you that a life without adversity is a life without character. The English oak is coveted by shipbuilders the world around because of what storms and strong winds have put into it. Only as we wrestle against the gales of opposition are we adding muscle to our spiritual lives.

My friend, how are you reacting? Like Elijah, are you saying, "I must die *sometime*, and it may as well be now"? There's a better course. Kneel before the great Burden Bearer who suffered disappointment and heartache and cruelty for the whole human race. Find in the light of His sufferings the best interpretation of your own.

. . . all things work together for good to them . . . who are the called according to *his purpose.* Romans 8:28

Webster's Encyclopedic Dictionary defines purpose as "The use for which something is intended; its reason for being."

Billy Sunday used to say, "Men fail through lack of purpose rather than lack of talent." In other words, poverty of purpose is worse than poverty of purse!

A West Coast doctor took a three-year informal poll of his patients to determine their predominant desire in life. Eighty-seven percent said they wanted peace of mind. That surprised me. I would have guessed that wealth would lead the list. (On second thought, who ever heard of a millionaire scheming to make another million after his doctor has given him only three months to live?)

If God has a purpose for each of His children, and I believe He has, what is your primary goal in life? If you gain it, will it outlast you?

Here we are, given but one opportunity in which to blight or bless our generation and those to follow, and too often we are not only selfish, but incredibly shortsighted in our goals.

The historian Edward Gibbon wrote many years ago about new Athens:

In the end, more than they wanted freedom, they wanted security. They wanted a comfortable life and they lost it all – security, comfort, and freedom. . . . When the freedom they wished for was freedom from responsibility, then Athens ceased to be free and never was free again.

Could this possibly be God's will for anyone? His purpose for your life? Your purpose for living?

I give unto them eternal life; and they shall never perish, neither shall any man pluck them out of my hand. John 10:28

One of the most bewildering by-products of our affluent society is insecurity. It manifests itself in many ways — demands for a guaranteed annual wage, expanded welfare payments and fringe benefits, higher Social Security benefits, and lucrative retirement plans.

Security, however, means different things to different people. To some it is a lifetime monthly check, to others a bullish stock market, to still others it is a little patch of mortgage-free dirt. But security, in its fullest sense, cannot be attained in this life. Everything we own is subject to instant depletion by an unforeseen vicissitude.

I am not at all surprised that many minds snap when hopes are centered solely in this life. The only people who have a right to be happy, calm, and optimistic are those who place their hopes in the world to come. This is real security.

Eternal life, you see, is a gift. If we buy things on the installment plan, they don't belong to us until we make the last payment. But gifts are different; they are ours from the moment we receive them. Jesus said, "I give to them eternal life," and millions of believers have gone into His presence secure in that promise.

Across the centuries, multitudes have embraced Christianity, knowing in advance that they were signing their own death warrants by becoming one of His. But they were not bent on security in this life. They were pilgrims on their way to a celestial city and they were anxious to get there.

They had found the only true security — *eternal security!*

If a man die, shall he live again? Job 14:14

Millions of dollars are spent annually on drugs, treatments, and special foods which give promise of retained or regained virility, a lessening of the aging process and a few additional years of life. Clothing styles and cosmetics are designed to camouflage one's nearness to the grave. Yet the Ultimate Step is never defeated, only postponed. Death is invariably the winner.

It is said that King Philip of Macedon, father of Alexander the Great, employed a palace servant to approach him every morning with the greeting, "Philip, remember that thou must die." While some may consider this morbid, I would say the king displayed rare courage and foresight.

Sadly, the institutionalized church has wandered away from its divine commission to prepare people for death. Instead, it is arduously occupied with providing social services which are of benefit only on this side of the grave.

From time immemorial, writers have referred to themselves and their fellow men as "travelers," and sometimes "pilgrims." Don't all travelers and pilgrims have a destination? Yet when the average person is asked about life after death, he is likely to become angry and retort, "I don't go for that religious stuff! I believe death is the end of the line."

Well, Jesus didn't believe that. Nor did the Bible writers. Nor do I.

A university graduate wrote back to his alma mater to complain that although it had imparted to him much valuable knowledge, he had learned nothing about life's most inevitable event—death.

Only the Christian faith offers a triumphant answer to the question of death and beyond. It tells us that far from being a "great negation," death is a gate which opens out on everything to which life looks forward. As D. T. Niles put it, "Death is not an end but an exit; not a blank wall but a door."

Said the French infidel Voltaire in his old age, "I hate life, and yet I hate to die." Paul, the apostle, said: "For to me to live is Christ, and to die is gain" Philippians 1:21. No wonder Christians can sing at funerals.